SIGNS OF THE TIMES

SIGNS OF THE TIMES

Seven paths of hope for a troubled world

Jean Vanier

Translation by Ann Shearer

DARTON · LONGMAN + TODD

First published in English 2013 by
Darton, Longman and Todd Ltd
1 Spencer Court
140 – 142 Wandsworth High Street
London SW18 4JJ

Published under licence from EDIZIONI SAN PAOLO s.r.l. –
Cinisello Balsamo (MI), publisher of the first edition in Italian,
Segni (2011).

This edition translated from the French edition by Ann Shearer.

ISBN: 978-0-232-53015-5

A catalogue record for this book is available from
the British Library

Phototypeset by Kerrypress Ltd, Luton, Bedfordshire
Printed and bound in Great Britain by Bell & Bain, Glasgow

CONTENTS

The Church has always had the duty of scrutinizing the signs of the times and of interpreting them in the light of the Gospel. Thus, in language intelligible to each generation, she can respond to the perennial questions which men ask about this present life and the life to come, and about the relationship of the one to the other. We must therefore recognize and understand the world in which we live, its explanations, its longings, and its often dramatic characteristics.

Gaudium et Spes 4:1[1]

INTRODUCTION

The Second Vatican Council breathed energy and hope back into the Church.[1] The 2500 bishops called together by Pope John XXIII returned to the origins of the Church to make abundantly clear the good news announced by Jesus to the poor: that he came to bring freedom to captives, sight to the blind and liberty to the oppressed. The council's closing message, addressed to the world in 1965, summarised its conviction like this:

> All of you who feel heavily the weight of the cross, you who are poor and abandoned, you who weep, you who are persecuted for

justice, you who are ignored, you the unknown victims of suffering, take courage. You are the preferred children of the kingdom of God, the kingdom of hope, happiness and life. You are the brothers of the suffering Christ, and with Him, if you wish, you are saving the world. This is the Christian science of suffering, the only one which gives peace. Know that you are not alone, separated, abandoned or useless. You have been called by Christ and are His living and transparent image.[2]

To the poor, the sick and the suffering[3]

L'Arche was born in 1964, before this declaration was made. But it was attuned to it. Until now, people with an intellectual disability[3] had been relegated to psychiatric hospitals or enclosed in their families. They were often considered 'mad', even 'non-people'. Sometimes their disability was seen as a sign of God's condemnation, attributed to a sin of their parents. Père Thomas Philippe, my spiritual father and the person who inspired me to start l'Arche, had been chaplain to a small institution. He had sensed the simple and trusting hearts of the institution's inhabitants, hidden behind their manifest difficulties and disabilities. He took heed of Paul's words: 'God chose what is foolish in the world to shame the wise, God chose what is weak in the world to shame the strong. God chose what is low and despised in the world, even things that are not, to bring to nothing things that are' (1 Cor 1: 27–28).[4]

The church is a body. It needs its weakest members and they should be honoured. Isn't this the message of Vatican II? Père Thomas had been an immediate enthusiast for the opening the Council had created, and above all for its vision of the Church as the people of God, with those who were the least powerful at its very centre. L'Arche's vocation was to stand solid with them, which is why it wasn't simply a question of welcoming people with a disability. It was a question of living together with them in the joy of helping each person, whether defined as handicapped or not, to grow in the true love that is rooted in wisdom. Today, we have more than 140 communities across the world, all living in the same spirit.

Without knowing which direction the Council was going to take, I had by now welcomed two men with an intellectual disability from a closed and violent institution, to share my life with them and help them live in freedom and dignity. What I hoped was to build with them a new kind of Christian community. A few years later, in 1971, Marie-Hélène Matthieu, who founded the Christian Office for People with an Intellectual Disability, and I organised a pilgrimage to Lourdes. This was designed to help such people to find their true place in the Church: we brought together four thousand people with a disability, four thousand parents and four thousand young supporters. That is how Faith and Light was born. Today, this community consists of 1500 communities in 84 countries, each one of them welcoming people with a disability, their parents and their friends to come together to celebrate, share and pray.

L'Arche and Faith and Light have led us to discover something wonderful: when we enter into a real relationship with people with an intellectual disability, we are transformed. These people, historically considered as humanity's least significant members, can show us the way to humanity's heights. When the Word of God descended into human flesh, it became small and weak. It divested itself of divine glory to lead us towards the Father. If we 'lower' ourselves to be with the weakest among us, then we meet the One who humbled himself for us all. Nearly fifty years of life in l'Arche and my participation in Faith and Light, all shared with people who are vulnerable, suffering and humiliated, have transformed me. They have led me to accept my own vulnerability and shown me how to exercise authority in a community by awakening the personal conscience of each of its members. These people with a disability, so apparently weak, have brought me to the heart of the Christian Mystery.

This book was born out of exchanges with a friend. Cristiana Santambrogio had been profoundly touched by life in one of our l'Arche houses and by the way in which its men and women, often profoundly disabled, are able to expand, become more and more aware of themselves as valuable individuals and journey towards an inner peace. They can do this because not one of them is shut up in a vision of being human which obliges them to espouse the so-called 'normal' contemporary values, like independence, success, achievement – the very values which mark them down as inferior. Our community life allows them to feel they truly belong and gives them the security to grow towards a genuine freedom to be themselves.

The values extolled by our wealthy modern societies often damage inner freedom and personal conscience. We live in what could be called a tyranny of normality. Of course norms and laws are necessary to provide human beings with a strong inner structure. But in our times, cultural normalisation based solely on success and power prevents us from becoming truly ourselves, with our strengths and weaknesses, and from developing what is at our heart. Even in the Church, isn't there a tension between the values of society and those of the Gospel?

The spirituality of l'Arche rests on the absolute principle which Vatican II emphasized so strongly: the profound value of each individual, whatever their culture, religion, way of life, ability or disability. This spirituality, reinforced both by the Word of God and by what we learn from the social sciences, is born from experience. It is through day to day life that we have learned what can help people who are fragile, or withdrawn into anger and depression, to become more human, more open to themselves and others. This spirituality is not cut off from humanity: it aspires to a growing love for others, and especially of those in need. St John is clear: 'He who does not love his brother whom he has seen cannot love God whom he has not seen' (1 Jn 4:20). And again: 'If anyone has the world's goods and sees his brother in need, yet closes his heart against him, how does God's love abide in him?'(1 Jn 3:17). We sing and pray: 'Where there is love and charity, God is present'. Real love and true relationship are signs of an authentic spirituality.

Jesus says to the elect: 'Come, O blessed of my Father, inherit the Kingdom prepared for you from the foundation of the world' (Mt 25:34). The elect are those who have lived in compassion and goodness towards the most destitute, whether or not they explicitly knew Jesus. L'Arche wants to be a school of love for all its members, both people with a disability and their assistants. Many of them have been led to become increasingly open towards God, their own Churches and respective religions, and to a spirituality which strengthens them in their love for the other.

It is through my own church that Jesus has called me to bring good news to the poor and proclaim the liberation of those who are captive and oppressed. I am grateful to the Church for the nourishment of the sacraments, for the word of God and for the inspiration given by the successor to Peter. I am far too aware of my own poverty, weakness and infidelity to judge anyone else for theirs. Nevertheless, I am disappointed by the loss of vitality and enthusiasm among members of my church which makes it hard for them to commit themselves to the poor so that they can bring them the good news of Jesus. Too few ecclesiastical authorities affirm that faith in Jesus is intimately bound to this commitment.

Are we enough aware of the one and a half billion people who live in gigantic slums, especially in South America, Africa and Asia? How can we fail to be horrified by this situation, especially when this population is growing by 100,000 a day?[5] The chasm between the rich and the poor is humanity's greatest drama. Weren't the disciples of Jesus called to work to fill in this chasm and make our societies more human? Because I love my Church, I am very attentive to all the signs of the presence of God and the work of the Holy Spirit in the hearts of the many men and women who, without knowing Jesus, are working to bridge the gap between the rich and the poor.

In his Epistle, St John affirms that his faith in Jesus is based in experience: 'That which we have heard, which we have seen with our eyes, which we have looked upon and touched with our hands concerning the word of life ... we proclaim also to you so that you may have fellowship with us' (1 Jn 1:1–3). I want these pages too to be based in the long experience of many people in our l'Arche communities. The people with whom we share daily life – who have so often been rejected and despised – are not God's 'poor little children' whom we have to look after. They have a special mission to humanity and to the Church. They have a gift to convey. They help us discover a new vision for society and for the Church.

It will take decades to see all the consequences of listening to the least powerful among us and allowing ourselves to be led by them. For now, I want to open some avenues for reflection and, following the invitation of Vatican II, to 'scrutinise the signs of the times'. But if the Church is to discover and live the riches the Council offers, if what the Holy Spirit is preparing is to come to birth, something defensive, in-turned and narrow in the Church's own vision today has to disappear. Since the Council, many have become afraid because the freedom and opening it announced have not always been lived within an inner renewal in the Holy Spirit. Jesus said: 'Fear not, little flock' (Lk 12:32). Perhaps we have to become humbler yet before his prayer for the unity of all Christians and all the men and women of the world can be realised.

This book was published in French in 2012. While the English version was being prepared, Pope Benedict XVI resigned and his successor, Pope Francis, began his ministry. In his first media audience, the new Pope explained why he had chosen that name. As soon as the result of the election had become clear, his good friend Cardinal Claudio Hummes, Archbishop Emeritus of Sao Paulo, had given him a hug and kiss and said 'Don't forget the poor!'

> And those words came to me: the poor, the poor. Then right away, thinking of the poor, I thought of Francis of Assisi … For me, he is the man of poverty, the man of peace, the man who loves and protects creation … How I would like a Church which is poor and for the poor![6]

At his inaugural Mass, Pope Francis called on men and women of goodwill to become 'protectors' of all creation, and spoke of his own role: ' [the Pope] must open his arms to protect all of God's people, and embrace with tender affection the whole of human-ity, especially the poorest, the weakest, the least

11

important ... the hungry, the thirsty, the naked, the sick and those in prison'.[7] And later, he hoped the joyful Easter message would go out to 'every house and every family, especially where the suffering is greatest, in hospitals, in prisons ...'[8]

Yes, the Holy Spirit is indeed preparing new things – maybe even a new and deeper vision of love, springing up from the hearts of those who have been rejected and who are craving for authentic relationships. Are we ready to respond?

CHAPTER 1

FROM HUMILIATION
TO HUMILITY

My starting point is one of the most immediate and pressing signs of the times: humiliation. And I want to reflect on it through an episode of history that remains equally immediate. Xavier Beauvais' 2010 film *Of Gods and Men* (*Des Hommes et des Dieux*), took us back to an episode which seems to offer a key to understanding the situation of Christians in today's world [1]. This film, which moved so many people so deeply, retold the tragic fate of nine Trappist monks of Tibhirine in Algeria, who lived in deep harmony with their Muslim neighbours until 1996, when Islamic fundamentalist forces ordered them to leave. Rather

13

than leave the people to whom they felt so close, they chose to stay. Two escaped the fundamentalist attack, but the other seven were kidnapped and murdered.

I am struck by how deep a sense of humiliation colonisation and decolonisation has left in Algeria. To speak of humiliation here is not to evoke a situation where there was a conscious intent to humiliate the other, in which there was one who was the humiliator and one the humiliated. The humiliation here was born of historical circumstances which produced a reversal, and it applies equally to any group, church or culture, previously dominant or at least recognised as such, which suddenly finds itself in the opposite position. Now it is wounded because it is despised, its human value no longer recognised, and it experiences this in a flood of shame, self- loathing, depression or anger. The sense of humiliation can become the more violent when the faults of this previously superior group reveal its own poverty and impotence. Its attempts to reclaim superiority show only its weakness, and these attempts seem more and more insulting to those who witness them.

The presence of the French in Algeria was beneficial in several ways: they built schools and hospitals and they did good works. But these came with the underlying message that the Algerians were incapable of doing such things for themselves. The humiliation felt by the Algerians transformed into anger, and then rebellion, and they demanded independence. The war in Algeria was violent; both sides used torture. The Algerians took power and the French fled, and this was a humiliation for them. Access to what the Christians had built up was closed; the Church, previously at the top of the social scale, now found itself at the bottom. The clergy was much divided, but mostly decided to leave. Only Cardinal Duval, Archbishop of Algiers, took a clear position and, together with those members of the Church who were working with the Algerians, accepted the new situation. The clarity of his stance was a great strength for the Church in Algeria, which was thus able to discover the importance of 'encounter'. Eventually this became possible on a person to person level, without the hierarchy of power, and in a respect for difference.

Today, the Church is experiencing humiliation as it retraces pages in its history when Christians acted in contradiction to the Gospel. The violence of the Crusades and their eventual failure was a humiliation, as was the terrible destruction of Constantinople in 1204. In the same way, each of the numerous internal ruptures which mark the history of Christianity left a deep wound, especially the separation of the Roman and Eastern churches in 1054 and the Reformation and the establishment of the Anglican Church, which meant that during the fifteenth and sixteenth centuries half the population of Europe left communion with Rome. Slavery is also written into these wretched pages: we should remember that from the beginning of the nineteenth century, the British Parliament mostly outpaced the Catholic Church in the struggle for abolition, thanks to the courage of William Wilberforce, a devoted Evangelical. Nor can we possibly ignore the fact of the Christian persecution of the Jews in so many ways and across the ages. We had to wait until 1965 and the declaration *Nostra Aetate* of Vatican II before a new way of relating between Jews and Catholics was inaugurated.

So today the Church does indeed experience humiliation, in the recognition that some of its historical actions have failed to accord with the Gospel. Many of these took place within living memory. The 1933 Concordat between the Holy See and the Third Reich, signed by Cardinal Pacelli and Hitler's representative, delivered German Catholics to the Nazi regime and the war for which it was preparing. In France, under the Vichy government, some bishops opposed giving the Eucharist to members of the Resistance: they accused these men and women of weakening, by their attacks on the German army, the only bulwark against what the bishops saw as the ultimate enemy of Christianity: Stalin's Russia. For this reason, the Church in France was largely *pétainiste*: few bishops had the courage to hold to another vision. In the same way, in later years, the Vatican supported fascist dictators like Pinochet in South America, which made it complicit with regimes whose messages were so contrary to its own.

17

The Church has too often been allied with temporal power, with rulers and the great landowners. And this is where its humiliations have begun, because these alliances are in such contradiction to the Gospel's message of the primacy of love and the honoured place of the least powerful. But has the Church been able to recognise this, or has it ascribed its own humiliations to betrayal by the 'other'? How do any of us behave in the face of humiliation? Do we recognise it, or blame others for betraying us? Would recognition not be a way towards growth in humility and a new encounter with our deepest selves – and from there to a deeper union with Jesus?

Pope Jean-Paul II shone a great light on this path towards humility. During his papacy, he invited the Church to become aware 'with a rekindled clarity, that all through history its faithful have been shown to be unfaithful, in their sins against Christ and the Gospel'.[2] He took many steps in search of forgiveness, most significantly the penitential Eucharist which he celebrated during the jubilee year of 2000. In the same way, the declaration of repentance by the

French bishops in Drancy in 1997, for the behaviour of the Church during the Nazi Occupation, was particularly revealing of the Church's capacity to stand in the truth when faced with humiliation. The declaration acknowledged that there had been no lack of courageous acts among Christians.

> But we must recognise that indifference far outweighed indignation …Given the magnitude of the tragedy and the incredible nature of the crime, too many pastors of the Church, by their silence, offended the Church itself and its mission. Today we confess that this silence was a mistake … This failure of the Church of France and its responsibility towards the Jewish people are part of its history. We confess this sin. We ask God's forgiveness and we ask the Jewish people to hear these words of repentance.[3]

Humiliation unrecognised leads to victimisation and a sense of outrage, even a straightforward refusal to look reality in the face. But if this is done, then there can be a true encounter with the other as an equal, person to person, and in mutual respect for difference. From here can come 'the sacrament of encounter' and 'the sacrament of brotherhood', of which Irenaeus first spoke in the third century, and which was taken up by other Church Fathers.

And here we return to the episode retold in the film *Of Gods and Men*, and the extraordinary key it offers to understanding the whole history of the Church. Christian de Chergé and his brothers chose to stay in their monastery despite the danger, because they were living a deep and true encounter with their Muslim neighbours. They did not stay because they were unaware of the danger, far from it, but because they had given their lives to God and to the Algerians, their brothers and sisters in humanity. And this could be what we as Christians are called to now: to live true encounters.

It is not just historically that the Church has known times of humiliation. Undeniably, it is living through another such period today. The lack of priests, the scandals that have erupted around paedophilia and the abuses perpetrated by Father Marcial Maciel, the founder of the Legion of Christ, are sad examples. (I will return to the issue of paedophilia.) But such humiliations can offer the opportunity for an examination of conscience similar to that lived through by the Church of Algeria, which brought a great change in the way church authorities were able to 'encounter' Muslims. Of course this examination will not be possible if the Church retreats into a rigid assertion that the only mission of Christians, whether priests or laity, is the 'conversion' of the other to its faith, or that the only way of 'doing good' to the other is to change them. The true mission is the opposite: to recognise our faults, and encounter the other with humility, respect and love, as Jesus did. The Christian faith is not an ideal divorced from reality: it is an encounter with Jesus which invites us to live our encounters with others in reality and humility.

In our contemporary societies, 'the good' is too often confused with success. 'Doing well' is reduced to receiving the approbation of others, in order to feel part of a certain social milieu. We are driven by the question 'What position can I have if I don't succeed?' Behind this question we can hear the fear that we will have no place at all, the fear of humiliation. This is what drives us to conform, in the hope that doing so will guarantee success. The experience of humiliation in the history of the Church teaches us something else: to look reality in the face with humility, to recognise our faults, and to search not to dominate but to serve.

In our l'Arche communities, we live with people who have been profoundly humiliated. I think of Pauline, whom we welcomed in 1973, when she was forty years old. She had epilepsy, diabetes, and hemiplegia, with a paralysed arm and leg; she was extremely violent. Her family and those around her had treated her with a certain scorn, as a 'cripple', a 'defective'. She was a disappointment to her family; she was unable to go to school. She had no right to speak for herself or voice her desires. So her furious outbursts were hardly surprising. Forty years of humiliation had led her to believe that she was worthless. Her violence was nothing less than a cry for life, a scream which seemed to say 'Will someone believe in me?' At l'Arche, through everyday life in her household, Pauline was finally heard, recognised and respected, with tenderness and humility. Thus, little by little, she was able to find peace and self-acceptance. She became more open to others in her turn, with the respect that she herself had been shown.

What are Christians to do when they find themselves humiliated? Julia Kristeva, the distinguished psychoanalyst and social philosopher, with whom I have worked a great deal on the idea of disability,[4] has often told me that she is ill at ease with the inconsistency of some Christians: their ideas put them on the political left, but their hands pull the financial reins firmly to the right. In response, I recalled with her a certain Claire de Favarone d'Offreduccio, the disciple, sister and friend of Francis of Assisi. She was destined to an aristocratic marriage in order to preserve and reinforce her family's power. Her uncles used social convention and force of arms as well to persuade her to accept this. But at 18 years old, Claire was able to escape the chains of 'normalisation', conformity and comfort, to follow Francis, the Poverello. This was a clash of two cultures: on one side, that of the Gospel and personal conscience and on the other, that of her social class, with its tyranny of success. The Offreduccio family were 'good Christians'. But Claire's flight 'humiliated' them. They accused her of betrayal, when in fact what she was doing was revealing their own inability to live the authenticity of their faith.

This ambivalence still runs through the Church and many of its members will be faced with it – for instance, when they are invited to follow the criteria of social success rather than the message of Jesus. Some churchmen find it hard to know which culture they want to belong to: that of the Gospel and humility, or the less uncertain one of social achievement, the approbation of superiors and the peremptory assertion of a certain Christian ideal which is divorced from reality. Without doubt, they are much influenced by the contemporary audio-visual culture, which carries this normative message of achievement. It is only human to want to believe in this message, and I am particularly touched by those who are thrown back on their own resources, without the support of a community. These priests live in great solitude and they can sometimes risk feeling lost. The danger for them is to take refuge in a certain cult of power and certainty, for fear of humiliation or of meeting people whose vulnerability mirrors their own. In daily life, such men actually find themselves completely powerless – unless they live in a remote village – and they can suffer profound problems of identity.

Even the role models presented to them by their own Church can appear surprising. Pope Benedict XVI for instance, chose to dedicate the priestly year of 2009 to the memory of the Curé d'Ars, with whom he associated Padre Pio. How could these two figures, belonging to a specific epoch, shed light on the road of contemporary churchmen? Of course it's no longer possible to live like the Curé d'Ars, waiting in a confessional until people come to you, any more than it is possible to live like Padre Pio, who was the recipient of quite exceptional graces. Yet these two men exemplify a path of humility and surrender to Jesus, a path of true encounter: their value is not as role models to be literally imitated, but as signs of the presence of Jesus. Isn't it to such priests that our societies should turn, those who are gentle and humble and bring a true presence to deep encounters, and reveal the goodness of Jesus?

Our society has a tendency to cling to models of power and to forget the strength that lies in humility. So, for instance, we have even come to elevate Mother Teresa into a superior figure. But actually, she was 'little' Mother Teresa. When I was asked to give a talk on 'blessed' Mother Teresa, my response was that she was a light for the world precisely because of her lack of grandeur. She once told me something which I consider an extraordinary sign for our times. Many Muslim and Hindu women wanted to join her Missionaries of Charity without becoming Catholics; some even wanted to create a Hindu group. Mother Teresa told me that she had received permission from

Rome to do this, and asked me if I would preach the first retreat for this group. I gladly accepted, but alas, nothing came of it. It is because of these crazy dreams of 'little' Mother Teresa that I can't speak of 'blessed' Mother Teresa. Her audacity and her hope for the unity of all human beings was that of a gentle and humble woman who dared to translate into reality the dreams in which she believed.

To place human beings on pedestals is to run the risk of no longer seeking them where they are, of no longer seeing where they have been and where they are today, which is hidden in God. The Church shows us a way towards them: we must look for Mother Teresa in the destitute and dying, in the streets, not anywhere else. The models we are given, the images of sanctity presented to us, throw us back once again into the conflict between the two cultures in our own lives: should we be presenting the 'achievement' of a Christian ideal or the Gospel? I believe that the true sign of sanctity today lies in the 'sacrament of encounter'. Faith is not the preaching of an ideal life, but above all a meeting with one person: Jesus.

The 'sacrament of encounter', like the 'sacrament of the poor', demands that we live in Jesus and He in us. This requires a transparency, a purification of our lives. We aren't here either to change or to convert the other. That is the work of Jesus, because faith is a gift of God and not an expression of power or superiority. We are here to encounter the other in humility, to respect them and to reveal their individual value. The 'sacrament of encounter' makes Jesus present. This encounter can only be possible between people who discover themselves as equals, capable of mutual trust and of receiving the gift of the other. Encounter reveals their value to the other and implies a listening with our whole being, without giving up our own truth or our personal conscience.

Vatican II had some essential things to say on this subject:

> In the depths of his conscience, man detects
> a law which he does not impose upon
> himself, but which holds him to obedience.
> Always summoning him to love good and

avoid evil, the voice of conscience when necessary speaks to his heart: do this, shun that. For man has in his heart a law written by God; to obey it is the very dignity of man; according to it he will be judged. Conscience is the most secret core and sanctuary of a man. There he is alone with God, whose voice echoes in his depths.[5]

These words have an amazing force. I cited them at a recent meeting, and I was astonished when a Christian told me that they had never heard talk of the personal conscience before. Why is this idea not given primacy? It will not become a substitute for the law, any more than it will negate the role of the Magisterium or the existence of objective truth. Conscience, as the example of Cardinal John Henry Newman showed us, is a light. The role of the Magisterium is to help Christians follow this light, to be true to it, and not to seek simply what pleases themselves or others.

This personal conscience is an aspiration towards the good, which can contradict that which appears 'appropriate' and 'normal'. It comes from inside and resonates like a call to live the truth of human dignity. Etty Hillesum, who died in Auschwitz and whose posthumously published diaries and letters describe her interior life in Amsterdam during the Nazi occupation, speaks of the 'inner voice': 'We seek in the other an instrument to cover the sound of our inner voice. If each of us listened only a little more to this voice, if we only tried to make it resound in ourselves, there would be a lot less chaos in the world'.[6] Each of us is free to recognise this voice, to decide whether to listen to it or not. Isn't it the voice which has urged so many men and women to stand out against falsehood, oppression and violence and to declare a road to freedom? Isn't it this voice which sometimes invites us to accept humiliation with humility rather than set out on the path of hate?

Today, as in the past, there are priests and lay people who reveal the face of Jesus. They live close to the poor, bringing them good news and liberating them from oppression of all sorts. Humiliation reminds us that the light may be veiled and the source of love may become invisible. It calls us to seek higher and further in order to discover the true meaning of the Church and to encounter Jesus more deeply, in his gentleness and his humility of heart.

CHAPTER TWO

FROM CONFORMITY
TO CONSCIENCE

The Church today is living the humiliation of the paedophilia scandals. Pope Benedict XVI was very clear about these: the most terrible persecutions experienced by the Church come not from outside, but from within, from its own sin, from the infidelity of its own members and their refusal to follow Jesus who came, with his gentle and humble heart, to teach us to live the true relationships that give life to others.[1]

How is the Church to live these times of humiliation? Does it even recognise them as such? Pope John Paul II's many pleas for forgiveness referred to in the previous chapter can help us think about this: he looked squarely at the sins and errors of governance of the past, and named the humiliations. But in spite of this example, there is still the temptation to seek loopholes: these were not the Church's misdeeds, for instance, but only those of bad Christians. This is to forget that the Church, source of life and grace, is made up of sinners. Its 'complex reality'[2] is not universally apparent; many people judge it by the actions of its members.

Paedophile priests bring a humiliation to the Church which must lead it to a deeper humility and greater wisdom. It is not enough to say that the problem can be considered resolved when these situations are reported to the police. Surely the Church must examine itself more deeply. Benedict XVI, in his book *Light of the World*,[3] raises the much wider question of the selection of future priests and their accompaniment. The theological and intellectual education they receive can obscure their equally indispensable need for education in relationship. They need to learn that true encounter demands humility, patience and listening. Alongside their intellectual training, they need an education of the heart.

An act of paedophilia is always an abuse of power and trust, whether committed by a family member, a teacher, a priest or a psychotherapist. In each case, the child has put their faith in someone in an accepted position of authority. And today, we seem to be seeking to emphasise the authority of the priest, and forgetting the listening, humility and vulnerability which are essential to true encounter. This is a time of humiliation, and any statement that doesn't resonate with that reality will grate like an intolerable lie. Until the situation is grasped and named, a pervasive sense of unease will continue. Humility? Humiliation? We say constantly that we must pray for humility. But it is much harder to pray for humiliation. Now we are living it. What are we to make of it?

At one level, paedophilia is a crime which cannot be covered up, but must be denounced, its perpetrators handed over to the criminal justice system. It is also, in the eyes of the Church, a sin. And didn't Jesus come to save sinners? I do not think that the condemnation of paedophile priests as forever unforgiveable will help them; far less will it resolve the problem of paedophilia in the Church. I believe that the issue has to be confronted in all its complexity, without trying to 'manage it' too quickly by conflating its distinct dimensions in a confusion of human, psychological, judicial, disciplinary, moral and spiritual approaches. Isn't it important to take time to foster acts of restorative justice, in which an encounter is carefully prepared between the abuser and the person abused? Then the one can ask for forgiveness and the other, perhaps in time, feel able to give it, so that together they can journey towards a true healing of the heart.

When I think of the passion of Jesus, I believe that his greatest suffering, even greater than his physical pain, was humiliation. If anyone is to live through this, the only thing they really need is a presence. This alone can assuage their pain and heal them. In re-reading the history of the Church in Algeria, we discovered that humiliation enabled it to find a relationship with the other that went far beyond any consideration of power and made possible a true encounter, in equality and humility. Now we see a reciprocal movement: when we are humiliated, we need a true presence at our side. I am often shocked, in representations of the Crucifixion, by the portrayal of Mary, Mater Dolorosa, at a distance of several feet from the Cross. At this moment, Jesus needed a very close, loving and trustworthy presence, because humiliation engenders a very specific human suffering, and a wound to the heart. The humiliated person needs that consoling presence which tells them: 'I am with you, I love you and trust you, and I give myself to be with you.' Through her heart, body and eyes, Mary offered this authentic presence, accompanying Jesus in his humiliation.

We are often afraid to look reality in the face. Here is just one example. I was supporting a priest who had fathered a child. He had had the courage – and I use the word advisedly – to leave the priesthood and his religious life, in full awareness of the gravity of his infidelity to his vows, in order to take responsibility for his actions. His order wanted his child to be adopted, and the child's paternity kept hidden, so that the priest could resume his religious and priestly calling. The culture of achievement, of 'ecclesiastical success', had brought pressure for concealment of a situation seen as humiliating for both the priest and his order. He however could step outside that culture: he preferred to carry the humiliation of being 'defrocked' and to assume his responsibility.

Considered as too heavy a burden by his religious order which could no longer look him in the face, this man became an outsider. His situation raises a further question: what kind of support had he been offered earlier? One of the great problems of our Church is its concern for its reputation and fear of humiliation. It is not alone in this. In *People of the Lie*, the American psychiatrist Scott Peck cites a psychiatric study, based on research and interviews, of disturbance among American soldiers who had killed civilians in the Vietnam War.[4] This study was never published, because it was considered too damaging to the reputation of the American army. Here is an example of how the norms of success and concern for public standing, what I call the 'tyranny of normalisation', can lead people who carry responsibility to live in contradiction: they want to keep up appearances while knowing the gravity of the wrongdoing which has been committed. Isn't truth the one thing that can set us free? And doesn't accepting the truth demand that we take the path of humiliation that can lead to transformation?

'Transformation' is a key word in any talk of humiliation and encounter. We Christians sometimes give the impression that our faith comes in a solid block: 'you either have it or you don't'. But faith isn't simply a matter of belief in dogma and regulation. To have faith is to believe in, place our confidence in, a person: for Christians, that is Jesus. Then this trust, and the friendship it engenders, evolves. It is a journey of growth, transformation, deepening and humility, which is accompanied by a love and a vulnerability that become more and more radical and take us further and further away from the idea that we know a superior truth. This fragility both attracts and frightens us. 'When I am weak, then I am strong', says St Paul (2 Cor. 12:10).

Everything about encounter lies in the realm of the heart, where we do not seek to be superior to the other. In our societies, the imperative of 'normalisation' seems to be all-pervasive: we have to be strong to supplant and change the other. We cannot accept being weak. But a true encounter implies acceptance of our frailty and the frailty of the other. St Peter, called to be the rock on whom the Church was built, was profoundly humiliated by the way in which he denied Jesus, and by his own weakness and fear. He had to grow in humility and openness. St Paul reminds us that love is first of all patient, kind, and without envy. It isn't boastful or arrogant, irritable or out for its own interests. It takes no delight in injustice, but rejoices in the right. 'Love bears all things, believes all things, hopes all things, endures all things' (1 Cor 13:4–7). This love is given us as we accept our frailty. It is the fruit of an encounter whose source is in God. It is a gift of God, this encounter where there is no more superiority or inferiority.

All true encounters must integrate frailty, including death, the mortality which is the ultimate human frailty. Here is what Etty Hillesum has to say, as she accepts the coming reality of the Nazi destruction of the Jews:

> I have come to terms with life ... [By which] I mean the reality of death has become a definite part of my life; my life has, so to speak, been extended by death, by my looking death in the eye and accepting it, by accepting destruction as part of life and no longer wasting my energies on fear of death or the refusal to acknowledge its inevitability. It sounds paradoxical: by ex- cluding death from our life we cannot live a full life, and by admitting death into our life we enlarge and enrich it'.[5]

Etty Hillesum's life, right up to her death at the age of 29, is a perfect expression of this paradox: the more we can integrate our death, the more alive we become. And I would go so far as to say that this death is not simply a physical one, the end of our bodily existence, but made up of a multitude of 'deaths' – of bereavements and set backs, losses and renunciations, and humiliations as well. Each grief that we can integrate, whatever its origin, can become a source of life.

What is this weakness that is strength which St Paul writes about and which we so dread even as we seek to find it? Think of the 'blessed weakness' of the baby. The mystery of every human being is that he or she begins life in a state of great fragility and vulnerability. In their early days, infants can survive only through a presence, an encounter and the tenderness that they evoke. This is why their vulnerability can be called 'blessed'. Moved by such fragility, the mother enfolds the infant in a tenderness which says: 'I love you. I love you as you are. If you cry in the night, however foolish you are, it doesn't matter; I will go on loving you just the same. You won't need to be strong or even see things as I do for me to love you.' This love is a celebration: the mother and her child are celebrating their communion. The heart of their relationship is the mutual confidence that is carried through smiles, laughter and play, through exchange of looks and tender physical care.

For a small child, the body communicates: the mother's love is expressed through a tenderness that passes essentially through the body. This is a relationship which is intensely physical and deeply spiritual at the same time. The psychoanalyst Julia Kristeva says that infancy is both pre-religious and pre-social. I would add that it is a time of a quite unique bond between two people – primarily the child and the mother, but also the father or another parental figure. It is as if this stage is the untiring repetition of the statement: 'You are my beloved son, you are my beloved daughter.'

Little by little, as children grow, they move towards normalisation. They learn to be sensible, to study, to do sport, to have friends, follow the rules, do as they're told and become what their parents hope and desire them to be. The child learns to follow ethical, familial and cultural rules or the ways of their social milieu. To survive, children do what is expected of them. They feel they have to enter this normalisation, to believe it when they are told: 'If you don't work at school, you'll never get on in life.' The criteria of achievement and of living they are offered are those of the prevailing social norms. Is their personal conscience taken into account?

There is also a tendency to impose a certain normalisation onto Christian life: we must go to Mass, catechism and so on. Fortunately, more and more families are now seeking to awaken their child's personal conscience. How is this conscience to be educated? How to dialogue with the child? Some parents are asking their children: 'What do you feel about it? What do you think is the right thing to do?' Sometimes we fail to treat children as people, assuming that they have neither their own conscience nor the capacity for dialogue. This fails to recognise the wealth of their hearts, their thirst for truth and justice. It risks pushing the child to become no more than an obedient member of a cadre. Parents often use promises to get their way, or play on their child's fears, rather than initiating a true dialogue. This understanding of 'education' fails to take account of the child's own person or conscience.

But parents can sometimes find it difficult to enter into dialogue with their child. One reason for this is the pervasive conviction that children shouldn't suffer. If, for instance, grandmother is dying, it is thought better not talk about it too much. But this denies the child an opportunity to learn about life's suffering, and that to be human is to suffer, whether from toothache or the death of a loved one. In the same way, children are encouraged not to ask too many questions. Thus family taboos grow up, for example around money. One day a couple came to see me to discuss their daughter, who was 17 and wanted more pocket money than they could afford. I asked them whether they had explained to her how they managed their finances, to show how much father and mother earned, the household expenses, the cost of running the car, the necessary savings and what was left over for day to day living. They said they hadn't dared: 'We have no right to worry a child of that age with such things'. But why not? I asked. This adolescent girl was of an age to understand the realities of her family's financial situation.

To think of education in terms of social norms can also touch on religious questions within families. Some parents who call themselves atheists feel that their child must be so too, and neither ask questions about religion nor discuss it. Some families who call themselves Catholics make attendance at Mass obligatory without questioning aspects of the behaviour or preaching of the priest. But where then are the opportunities to cultivate the personal conscience? A friend who is a priest told me about hearing the confessions of several children who accused themselves of lying. He asked why. They all told him that their fathers had been furious when they told them about bad marks at school; from then on they'd been afraid to tell the truth. The priest rejoiced, because he had been able to create a place of encounter and trust, where the personal conscience of each child could be evoked. Such places are extraordinary.

The text of *Gaudium et Spes* about conscience, quoted in the previous chapter, seems to me essential. The question it raises is not about whether or not to follow the Magisterium, but about the education of the personal conscience, so that it can discern how best to act in truth, and above all in love for the other and the poor and disadvantaged. Today, faced at this very moment with this beggar I meet in the street or that person with a profound disability, what is the right response? It is my answer to that question which will guide my conduct. If my norm is the Gospel, then it is for my personal conscience to tell me how to live that norm, with prudence, in the concrete situations of everyday life. The Magisterium doesn't have anything to say about how to behave towards the person in front of me now. The personal conscience is much deeper than this law or any general norm laid down by the Magisterium, because it operates in concrete reality, where each situation is unique. We need to cultivate it by listening to the little 'interior voice' that Etty Hillesum writes about. It is through this voice that Jesus speaks and can sometimes lead us to actions which go against what appears to be conventional and 'normal'. Learning to listen takes a great deal of discernment and training.

When a child reads the Gospel, they understand that Jesus asks that we love each person, including our enemy, and that we do not judge them but forgive them. So what happens when, for example, they hear at mealtimes their parents disparaging Muslims, people on welfare benefits or immigrants? If the child cannot listen to their own conscience and their own inner voice, they risk living in a state of deep contradiction, which can lead them to stifle their conscience even further.

If families and priests do not teach children to listen to their own conscience, they will not grow up to be truly free adults: they will be content to do what others want, acting according to the norms rather than personal truth and love. I have often seen this illustrated through the parents of young assistants who came to l'Arche for a short time and then chose to stay. The parents were delighted when they first came, because this fitted with their criteria of a 'good deed'. But they were a lot less delighted when their children stayed. 'We spent so much on your education and you choose to live with people "like that"!' The story of Francis of Assisi and Claire d'Offreduccio, so strongly confronted by the tyranny of their familial and social norms, repeats itself across the centuries.

Norms establish a distinction between those who are 'good' and those who are not: they define the elite towards which to aspire. Prisoners, alcoholics, drug addicts, prostitutes? Let's have nothing to do with them! So it is easy to divide the 'good' from the 'bad', and from there 'good people' from 'bad people', just as it is easy to divide the 'normal' ones from the 'abnormal'. Our personal conscience however allows us to consider each person as they are, to respect them and to love them with their own individual history. So we can turn with goodwill and compassion towards the person with a disability, the person who lives on the streets or the one in the grip of an addiction. From here, we become able to see their suffering and not simply their 'abnormal situation'.

Priests and catechists insist on the religious norms: go to Mass, pray morning and night, participate in the sacraments. They sometimes forget that these norms are intended precisely to help us develop personal conscience and to live as Jesus lived, allowing ourselves to be drawn towards the good and the true. This is not emphasised enough. Once more, we can remember the experience of the Church in Algeria. When the Church is 'successful', its priests can be tempted to content themselves with being well-educated and competent in directing a parish, and forget that they are also there to radiate love. Then the sacrament risks becoming no more than a ritual, empty of meaning. But when the priest is deeply bound to Jesus, 'the sacrament of encounter' allows the other to be truly seen, as a precious being. Then the priest will see the other through the eyes of Jesus, humbly and lovingly, attuned to their being and their suffering.

The Church's social doctrine recognises each human being in their uniqueness and respects their differences; it remembers that from those to whom much has been given, much will be asked. The way of salvation is thus associated with the power to give and to work for justice. Benedict XVI emphasised that for a Christian, social action also demands above all a development of the heart. So is he not encouraging us to go further towards meeting the other in their need? It isn't just a matter of willingly doing good, but of helping the other to discover their personal value, and working with them to create a more just and loving world. It is a matter of encounter and of allowing ourselves to be transformed through that. A meeting with someone who is homeless, disabled, or an outsider, sharing the scraps of our lives with them, can appear difficult and even useless. But this can become the encounter which transforms us, leading us to the essence of what it is to be a person. The sacraments of the Church are there to lead us to love for the rejected and an encounter with them. Benedict XVI, in reference to John Chrysostom, said that the sacrament of the altar and the 'sacrament of the poor' constitute two aspects of the same mystery.[6] It is through these two sacraments that there is the true encounter with Jesus, and this encounter transforms us. The sacrament of the altar, the Eucharist, is fulfilled in the 'sacrament of the poor' – which means an encounter with Jesus in the poor. Isn't this what Benedict XVI was saying in his encyclical *Deus Caritas Est*? 'A Eucharist which does not pass over into the concrete practice of love is intrinsically fragmented'.[7]

CHAPTER THREE

FROM EXCLUSION
TO ENCOUNTER

An encounter is not an exercise in power. Nor is it a demonstration of generosity through which we seek to 'do good to' the other. It demands real humility and deep vulnerability. To be present to the other, to listen to them and regard them with respect and attention, allows us to receive in our turn. This is a communion of hearts – a reciprocal gift, freely given. In the course of my life, I have realised that people with great difficulties are really yearning for true encounters. One assistant in a l'Arche community was formerly involved with people working as prostitutes. One day, she arrived just in time to put her arms round a young man she knew, who was dying of an overdose. And this is what he said to her: 'You have never accepted me as I am. You always wanted to change me!' This woman had never truly encountered this young man. How could she really become a friend to someone caught up in drugs and prostitution? How could she recognise him as someone deeply wounded and reveal to him the beauty of his nature that was hidden behind his human poverty and addiction? His words worked on her as a revelation of what she was trying to protect herself from, but which was in fact central to her commitment.

The father who telephoned me one day to ask for help told a similar story. He was at his wits' end. His son, who was about forty years old, was alcoholic, and his wife had left him; he had had several stays in rehabilitation centres, but each time he came home, he started to drink again. This is what I told the father: He could, for a start, and within the family, stop speaking of his son as 'a problem', but recognise him as a man who was weeping. Then I suggested that he and his son, who didn't want to join Alcoholics

Anonymous, together sought out a friend with whom he would not drink, but go to the cinema or do some sport, speak or be silent, someone who would see him as more than a 'depressive alcoholic' and help him discover for himself what lay behind his depression and alcoholism. But of course, who wants to be friends with an alcoholic? Who wants, or is capable of, a real encounter with him? To become a real friend to wounded people, we all need the support of a community, in which we can reflect, discuss the difficulties and draw on the expertise of psychologists, doctors and others. True encounter is a shock to our ego, it throws us into our own impotence. To live it, we have to recognise our own weaknesses and our own need for help.

These two examples show how hard it is truly to encounter people seen as 'the lowest of the low' in the beauty of their person. Their histories are often very complex, often scarred by their suffering within their families. Each true meeting exposes us to our own vulnerabilities. 'Doing good to' allows us to keep our power, but in a true encounter we lose all power and all preconceptions. This demands a great deal of humility and growth towards love based in wisdom and prudence. We don't always know how to manage our own emotions, our instincts towards aggression or attachment, or our fears. Each one of us is fearful, each one of us is often ignorant of what we should say or do. So we begin to need others who can reassure and heal us – a community, professional support, the Holy Spirit. True encounter impoverishes us and forces us to live our own poverty. This opens extraordinary perspectives for us: the meeting with the person who is poor, humiliated and rejected can transform us and show us the deep meaning of our life. Isn't this the road on which many assistants at l'Arche and Faith and Light are travelling?

The encounter between 'Mamie' and Peter offers an illustration of this journey. The woman we called Mamie was 80 years old. Her name was Françoise and she was profoundly disabled, blind and bedbound in the La Forestière, one of the houses at l'Arche. Peter was a young Canadian whose job it was to look after her. There was a whole period of mutual assessment.

Then one day, when Peter was feeding her, Françoise put her hand on his and turned her face towards him with a radiant smile. Peter later told me that he had never had such an experience: 'Suddenly, something changed in me. I discovered that Mamie (and you could not imagine someone more disabled) was attracted to me, that she loved me. In her own way, she was saying "Thank you". I had the experience of being no longer admired, but loved.' Peter in fact was not doing something 'admirable', but had entered into a relationship of love and tenderness, in which the other was recognised, not possessed. In the mutual gaze between these two people, one of whom was blind, there had been an exchange that said, 'I love you as you are'. To love someone is to reveal to them their profound beauty and so to help them reveal it to themselves. When Peter sensed that he was recognised by Françoise, he discovered his own deep value.

The more we become a friend to someone vulnerable and humiliated, the more we become a friend of God. Thus we experience what it is to be unique.

Françoise is unique because she shelters in the core of her being the sanctuary where God resides: that personal conscience where, in the words of *Gaudium et Spes*, each person is 'alone with God'.[1] Francoise revealed to Peter that he is unique, that he is loved simply for who he is.

I was once asked what were the deepest motivations for living at l'Arche. The principal motivation? Essentially, it's pleasure. For Aristotle, pleasure and joy are identical. In current parlance, we devalue pleasure; joy sounds more spiritual. But according to Aristotle, pleasure or joy are to be found in activities which unfold spontaneously, naturally and without difficulty. The more beautiful the activity, the more it brings pleasure and joy. If I am learning to play the piano, at first I find it tiring; then when I can play Bach or Mozart with relative ease, I feel a tremendous amount of pleasure. This pleasure is the feeling of being alive which flows from an activity that is going marvellously well.

This all seems simple, but the reality can be more complex. If, for example, an excellent musician is having a conflict with his wife then, behind his pleasure in the music, he may feel hurt, angry or ashamed. The pleasure he gains in his activity may be a way of fleeing from the reality of his relationship. This is why Aristotle's vision doesn't seem to me entirely adequate. True pleasure or joy can only spring from an action that is really unifying and peace-making for the individual, one in which they can engage fully, without splitting off or fleeing from more difficult aspects of themselves. Aristotle's partial definition may have stemmed precisely from his difficulty in defining what constituted 'a person'. For him, to be a person meant having *logos*, 'rational intelligence'. But he failed to take account of what we could call the human heart. Yet it is the heart which is the core of the person and the place of true encounter. And our attraction to the good and towards a life of truth finds its source in the heart, which has been awakened through the infant's communion with the mother.

If there is a discrepancy between this core of the individual and their activities, there can be no experience of profound joy. The greatest joy is an expression of unity with oneself. It can be a pleasure to play the piano, but playing can only become true joy if it stems from a deep integration of the person. Then music can be the best channel through which to express this deep sense of inner unity – something which all the greatest musicians must surely have experienced,.

Where does this integration come from? Real joy presupposes freedom, which in turn implies that we have named and accepted our fears. The greatest fear, even greater than the fear of death, is that of being humiliated. We dread that the other will see our weaknesses, our incapacities and our impotence, and that they will then judge us as beneath consideration. This evokes unspeakable shame and guilt which in turn may stem from rejection in childhood, sometimes by the very mother whose role it is to awaken the heart.

Julia Kristeva tells the following story. She was working psychoanalytically with someone who had a slight physical disability. This man was extremely successful: after his studies, he had become a trade unionist. But in his dreams, he heard a voice which harangued him: 'Shame, shame, shame!' Through his analytic work he realised that all his success was an attempt to flee this terrible sense of shame. Where did it originate? His parents had been ashamed of him because he wasn't 'normal', and thus he became ashamed of himself because he was 'different'. His life was a long battle with himself as he struggled to hide from his shame in order to find recognition.[2]

To feel we count as nothing in the eyes of others throws up some of our deepest anguish. When we are faced with something dangerous, we feel fear. But anguish is deeper and more diffuse than that: it is existential. We dread being completely lost, no longer knowing who we are. Humiliation has the power to evoke this feeling: we experience ourselves as utterly worthless but dare not acknowledge it, because we live in a world that demands 'normality' and achievement. It is at this deepest level that we need to find liberation. We flee from the feeling that we are worthless into superficial pleasures and joys, in which we can feel recognised. Julia Kristeva's patient had succeeded professionally and been recognised for it. But buried in his deepest self, he still carried something intolerable which he couldn't express and which denied him happiness. He could take no pleasure in who he was, because he was unable to accept himself as loveable. Only a true encounter with someone who loved him in both his strengths and his weaknesses would have enabled him not just to accept himself but to experience a transformation which would liberate him from shame. Saints who experienced this anguish in which they felt lost to themselves sometimes called it the dark night of the soul. They endured it by clinging to their faith in the God of love.

Jesus himself experienced anguish because he would undergo bodily death. This anguish is hard for us to understand. The Gospel tells us 'The Word became flesh' (Jn 1:14). This means that Christ was actually incarnated in human flesh, that his body was not an accessory that he could put on or leave off at will. His body was part of his identity. So with his death, the Word would lose its bodily agency, its expression through human flesh. This was a terrible anguish for Jesus: it was as if the Word itself was at risk of being severed in two. His body was part of the identity of Jesus, and his identity as Messiah meant that he was sent to bring good news to the poor and dispossessed. How can we too bring them news that is truly good? It is not by telling each person: 'God loves you'. It is by saying 'I love you in the name of Jesus'. That is what it means to be present to them in the flesh, because it was in the flesh that that Jesus was present to the poor and told them 'I love you' in the name of God.

So something essential would be ruptured by the death of Jesus. His body would remain united with the Word even in the tomb, but was no longer active in this vocation of conveying the love of God to the poor. Of course Jesus would always remain the Son of God, in union with the Father. But the rupture of death plunged Jesus into a state of deep anguish that it is impossible for us to seize and fully express. Mary – she who had given Jesus bodily form – had to be at the Cross, at his side in his anguish and humiliation. It seems impossible to me that she could have remained weeping at too great a distance. She had to be close to Jesus, close to his body, to convey to him 'I love you'.

What is it that we need most in the world? It is not to be 'normal', but to be loved. We need to know that there is someone who believes in us despite all our weaknesses and failings, and respects our personal secret. This recognition is a communion, an encounter and a presence which is carried through the flesh and through tenderness. The deepest joy is that which comes from feeling loved and recognised just as I am, in communion with another. I emphasise 'as I am' – that means with all my history, my gifts and my fears, with all my weaknesses and even my sins. This is the way God loves me, sinner that I am, with my addictions, compulsions and my flights from myself. When I feel this love I experience a joy I have never yet known: I am loved, I matter to you.

How can I explain that despite all that is wounded in me, in my heart of hearts I remain in communion with God? True joy comes with communion. To live the 'sacrament of encounter' in humility brings absolutely no benefit. What use could there possibly be in becoming the friend of someone who is homeless, or of Mamie? None whatever. The only value is in the joy of communion and of presence. This encounter is transforming. This pleasure gives me a sense of truly existing and a meaning to my life, without my having to do anything at all. Where does this joy come from if not the discovery that the other loves me beyond any criteria of success or failure?

Communion with someone who has been humiliated thus opens me to the infinite; it enables me to touch that which is greater than either of us. This communion springs from something far beyond any notion of 'normalisation'. It is even an 'abnormal' experience, because it is beyond all norms, purely personal, truly unique. Where does the transformative power of such communion come from? It makes us discover that we are loved at a level far higher than all the defensive barricades we have built around ourselves to appear strong and recognised. So we experience the essence of our being, which opens us to communion with the Trinity.

This transformative power is beyond words, impossible to demonstrate. It can only be experienced. We are thrown into a reversal which reveals to us our own deepest identity: the part of us which we wanted to keep secret discovers that it is loved by the other. There is nothing in this experience that helps us either to earn more or climb the career ladder: it simply reveals to us the pleasure of being alive and free. So we open ourselves to an encounter where God is present. This experience is what is talked about in Chapter 25 of Matthew's gospel. Through compassion and humility, we discover Jesus in the poor. 'Truly I say to you. As you did it to one of the least of these my brethren, you did it to me' (Mt 25:40). Thus the sacrament of the poor becomes the sacrament of encounter.

This experience of transformation and self-revelation is not definitive. It is a starting point, a new beginning towards growth and truer love. I have discovered the presence of God in my presence to the other. This moment of shared communion is not explicable and can even seem absurd. But the moment when Mamie, who was blind, and Peter truly saw each other was a beatitude. Will a new road open from such experiences? For St Paul, the experience of encountering Jesus was so strong that it turned him completely inside out: he fell, he became blind, and he was transformed. He discovered his true self that had been hidden behind his hatred of Christians. For Paul, this was a beginning, a starting point. Many assistants at l'Arche and Faith and Light who have experienced this communion with someone who is profoundly disabled see it as a call to continue a journey of growth in love. They have understood that their hierarchical view of society, based in the criteria of normality, was false. Truth does not lie in 'success'. It is hidden in the hearts of the vulnerable.

How can we cultivate this initial experience? That is the mystery of each person. Peter lived a moment of beatitude; he was met above and below the barricades that surrounded his heart, and for an instant they crumbled. It was as if God was incarnated in him, in the most vulnerable part of his being; he lived an experience of God at a far deeper level than that of reason and so touched the depth of his own being. Through the love of Mamie, he had known himself to be loved by God. For Etty Hillesum, our role in a world where God is rejected is to protect his house in ourselves and tend its growth. 'One thing is becoming increasingly clear to me ... You cannot help us, but we must help You and defend Your dwelling place in us to the last'.[3] After a true experience of God, something is changed. Then it is a matter of continuing along this path towards a greater transformation.

Transformation, like the transfiguration of Jesus on Mount Tabor, leads us back to the plain (Mk 9: 2–9), back to everyday life. Now that we are set on the road, the struggle begins. I am struck by how we can bring together the Gospel of St Matthew and that of St John. In Matthew, Jesus, like Moses, brings back from the mountain a new direction for living: the Beatitudes, the law of poverty (Mt 5). In the Gospel of John, Jesus climbs the mountain, then sits down and gives the new law (see Jn 6.3): 'He who eats my flesh and drinks my blood abides in me, and I in him' (Jn 6:56); or as he explains this elsewhere, 'Abide in my love' (Jn 15:9). The great Beatitude is to eat the flesh of Jesus and drink his blood; the new path, which leads to a mysterious equivalence with him, is to abide in him. Our joy lies in becoming like Jesus, like God – not as a right but through a new gift. Joy lies in the communion in which we abide in Jesus as he abides in us. This gift is the beginning of an experience which we should follow with perseverance, struggling against all our egocentricities so that we can dwell in Jesus to become artisans of peace and unity in this broken world.

So transformation is an experience which opens up a new path, on which we become less and less governed by the fear of not succeeding, of insignificance, of losing ourselves entirely. This is the path of the 'perfect joy' of Francis of Assisi, who often experienced humiliations, and thus discovered the deepest parts of himself. We have to accept the grief of having neither high status nor a major responsibility, of not being recognised for what we do. And we have to accept simply being where we are free. This path will only end with our actual death, which is a passage to another life. Someone asked me if I am afraid of death. 'Not now', I replied. 'But ask me again a fortnight before it happens. Just now I have enough humiliations to be going on with!'

A child who has been beaten, abused or abandoned must build thicker and thicker walls of self-protection: life itself has to be defended. These walls may one day make it possible for him to become a head of the Mafia – or one day they may fall so that he can discover his true identity. A friend who works in palliative care in the United States told me about one of his patients who had cancer of the oesophagus, and had indeed been a Mafia boss, but was now in prison. This man had been abused as child, so the adult world was a threat to him; he had to become stronger than anyone else and ready to kill to defend himself. He could never afford to appear weak: being strong was his normality. My friend the doctor had to be very gentle with him to persuade him to accept any medical care. But in the course of his cancer, he became progressively weaker and his defensive walls crumbled. These two men, patient and doctor, became friends: as he became frail, the sick man could discover his own deep identity through becoming someone's friend. So weakness was no longer something to be rejected: it could become a path to living the joy of friendship.

When we can accept them, our humiliations and griefs can lead us into a process of transformation, just as can encounters with the weakest and most humiliated people, wretched of the earth. When our internal barricades fall, we feel the anguish from which they have been protecting us. But now too we are able to perceive a presence, the presence of the friend who loves us and who lives at our side. Of course it is hard to accept the times of anguish. But it is through them that we can find what is most beautiful and true in our own selves.

This is the road Jesus took: he lived the humiliation of the Cross. But unlike us, he never submitted to the tyranny of normality. In his bond with the Father he was entirely a loving and a wounded heart. Jesus was unique: the only person ever who was not wounded in his childhood by a lack of love. All of us were wounded to one degree or another, and so we seek to grab hold of and monopolise the other. Jesus never clings to people, and because he himself is all love, he is wounded when his love is rejected. This love is made manifest in his desire for each of us to be freed from our fear of loving. 'Behold I stand at the door and knock; if anyone hears my voice and opens the door, I will come in to him and eat with him, and he with me' (Rev 3:20). We can hear what he is saying here: 'If you don't want to be my friend – because you are too frightened, or because you don't know what it will lead to, or you are addicted to something else – I will just go on standing here and waiting for your "Yes".' So Jesus reveals his humility and the deep wound to his heart, to his loving self. He will go on standing outside and waiting for the 'Yes' which will allow him to come and live in us, so that we may truly love and welcome those who are 'different' and rejected.

To talk about exclusion touches me very deeply. It is one of today's terrible realities. There are a billion and a half women and men living in the great slums and shanties of the world, often tyrannised by different mafias. There are so many abandoned children who become criminal just to survive. There are so many men and women in prisons across the world. Who wants to encounter them? Who is ready to set out on the road of transformation?

CHAPTER FOUR

FROM POWER
TO AUTHORITY

In the Gospel of the beloved disciple, the word 'sign' is crucial. According to St John, Cana was the 'first of the signs'. It is 'signs' which reveal that Jesus has been sent by God. A sign means a great event which is visible and reveals a presence of God. To see signs, we have to be alive to reality, to what is actually happening. We have also to rid ourselves of prejudices, or at least keep them in check, so that we can experience reality's full force. Isn't sin to be found in ideologies which prevent us from seeing signs? If we cut ourselves off from experience and signs, we will be unable to see the presence of God.

The leaders of the Jews were fixed in their ideas about God. Their false reading of the signs led them to say that someone who cured a blind man on the Sabbath could not be sent from God. This experience went against their ideology. They accused Jesus of going against the Law. But the sign takes us out of our supposed 'knowing' or our false interpretations, to introduce us to a reality inhabited by God. What is it to 'know'? In his dialogue with Nicodemus, the leader of the Pharisees who 'knows' many things, Jesus leads him to accept that the wind blows where it wills, 'but you do not know whence it comes or whither it goes' (Jn 3:1–8). Nicodemus came to Jesus because he *saw* the signs that said Jesus had come from God. But he could not fully accept that Jesus was sent by God. When what we 'know' about God, when our certainties, 'truth', theology and vision of the world are opposed to experience, we are in danger of missing a truth that God wants to show us.

If we are to grasp this truth, we need to recognise the signs of God in the world today. Vatican II reminds us:

The Church has always had the duty of scrutinizing the signs of the times and of interpreting them in the light of the Gospel. Thus, in language intelligible to each generation, she can respond to the perennial questions which men ask about this present life and the life to come, and about the relationship of the one to the other.[1]

These signs can be of different kinds. The fact that so many people saw the film *Of Gods and Men*, which I discussed in Chapter 1, shows us that the life and death of those seven monks are a sign of God's care for our times. For me, this film reveals God's presence.

Another sign of the times was Benedict XVI's visit to Great Britain in September 2010. All the commentators predicted catastrophe; many critics said his visit would be counterproductive. But when Benedict addressed Parliament, he received a standing ovation. What had happened? Surely this man, on this occasion, had allowed a light to shine through him which went beyond the current order of things. He had been a sign of the humility and luminosity of Jesus in a citadel of our secularised societies.

I believe too that Etty Hillesum was a sign of God's compassionate presence in the midst of the Shoah and the concentration camps. This young Jewish woman, so psychologically fragile, lived a progressively more real experience of God which transformed her heart. In her journal she shows us a path, in the midst of the most appalling suffering, towards human maturity and towards God. She shows us the strength of personal conscience in a despairing world.

Another sign of God's presence in our world is the community of Taizé, founded by Brother Roger Schutz. This place is the image of Jesus crucified, arms outstretched to all Christians, all churches, all young people who are in search of the truth. It is the manifestation of Jesus who says: 'Come to me, all who labour and are heavy laden, and I will give you rest' (Matt. 11:28).

In our societies, dominated by the tyranny of normality and governed by laws which are sometimes passed without any reference to an ethical vision of human beings, our conscience is in danger of being sunk in subjective desire for success or superficial enjoyment. The Magisterium can be necessary to objectify our view of complex moral and ecclesiastical questions, particularly around life and death. But it does not dictate our actions in day to day concrete reality. What then should we do to become aware of the signs of God for our time? Here we touch on the challenges of education. Will we simply send our children to study, or will we also take them to places where they will meet people excluded from everyday life, so that they can learn to ask questions and appreciate reality? The world we live in is not ideal. Our education systems tend to develop the head with ideas and laws; they forget to help the child engage with the reality of the world, with personal discernment and openness to every person. The reality confronting a child today is far greater than that of their social class or particular group. Children have to be allowed to look about them and discover the importance of each human being – through visits to prisons, for instance, or meetings with people of different cultures. At l'Arche, we have taken care to develop training for assistants based in their own experience, which helps them become aware of their own difficulties and fears when faced with people who are fragile and vulnerable. This enables them to respond through a healthy understanding of both human nature and the Word of God. This dialogue between their personal experience and God's word is an education of their personal conscience.

Signs appeal to the personal conscience, which is at the service of life and love; they call us to live more in God and allow us to give life to others. For Christians, it is clearly the Gospel which is the basis of an educated conscience: the love of God and our neighbour. But only conscience can discern what is just in a specific context, and what God is asking of us so that we can truly love people who are different from us. Conscience is like the voice of God which shows the way of love in the here and now.

Christians express their confidence in God. But they are often fearful of affirming confidence in themselves and their personal conscience. True self-confidence is a sign of respect for the child of God that we are, called to do beautiful things for Him. We cannot love others if we do not love ourselves. We have to help each person to love and respect themselves and to have confidence in their own conscience and in the Holy Spirit who gave it to them. Jesus calls us not to judge, but to see the other as our sister or brother, through the eyes with which God sees them. This is also true for ourselves. Sometimes we prefer to forget that God is telling us 'You are my beloved child', because that means that we need to make an effective response! To know ourselves loved by God is not to exonerate us from becoming aware of our compulsions, our fears, our wounds and our culpability. But in his love, God invites us to leave these behind and to follow our conscience, in the light of the Holy Spirit.

At l'Arche, I see how many assistants can lose self-confidence. They are so quick to see the negative in themselves because of their difficulties in relationships with people with different disabilities. Assistants need support and affirmation if they are to discover and keep on discovering their own essential worth and beauty, their capacity to love in truth and live according to their own conscience.

This leads me to make the distinction between power and authority. Power imposes, it is the capacity to influence and modify the other through bypassing or crushing their conscience. Authority is linked to growth, a type of power which can help people develop their own sense of responsibility, their creativity, their personal conscience and their freedom. In his image of the good shepherd, St John helps us make this distinction between power and authority (Jn 12: 11–18). The first characteristic of the good shepherd is to know each member of their flock by name. In the same way, the person who exercises authority will know the strengths and weaknesses of each individual. This listening to and knowledge of the other – and especially of people who are most vulnerable – leads to mutual confidence and makes possible a relationship of communion. The good shepherd is called to attract and to lead each person towards the light of truth. The goal is to help them develop their personal conscience and freely discover their purpose, and to recognise their own human dignity and grow in maturity and inner freedom. The shepherd is able to sacrifice their own interests, time, and even their life to this goal.

This does not mean protecting people from challenges, mistakes and suffering. Julia Kristeva says something important for people in positions of authority and who accompany those who are discovering the meaning of their life: the pleasure of encounter only exists in so far as it can integrate the experience of death. Authority knows how to mourn the death of its own projects for the other: 'You are you, you have your own road to follow, your own unique vocation and it is different from mine'. This recalls the last page of St John's gospel, where Peter sees John, the beloved disciple, and asks Jesus: 'Lord, what about this man?' Jesus's reply, to the man to whom he has just entrusted his entire flock, is astonishing: 'If it is my will that he remain until I come, what is that to you?' (Jn 21:20–23). This means: 'You are you, you have your mission, but John also has his, and it isn't for you to know that or to decide what it should be. Your role as shepherd is to have an infinite respect for the vocation of each individual, which only their personal conscience, illuminated by the Holy Spirit, can dictate'. And to Peter, Jesus adds: 'Follow me!'

Laws are necessary to give structure to human beings. They should be clearly explained and openly stated. So if Pauline wants to hit out at someone, she must know that this is not allowed, that there is a sanction against it. Because violence can invade the heart, clear limits must be put in place. It is power that formulates these limits, it is authority which says that each person is called to grow and to develop in self –confidence. The father is often said to be the one who teaches the child about limits. If the child disobeys, the mother sometimes appeals to this paternal role: 'You deal with it!' True authority passes through mutual listening and dialogue, taking the law as a starting point. Paternity can't be limited to declaring the law and making the child respect it; it also encourages the growth of conscience towards personal maturity. Authority has to remember that the first law is the law of love, compassion and kindness.

This is why acts of power, necessary as they are if there is refusal to dialogue, need to be accompanied by understanding of the other, which confirms what is good and true in them. How can power be exercised as an expression of love which encourages growth? If I order Pauline to stop hitting other people, it isn't enough simply to state the law: 'That isn't done! And that's it!' I have to talk with her: 'Why did you do that? It's important that you understand what it feels like to the other person. It really has to stop: violence solves nothing. But remember the times when you were happy to be around other people? We both know that you can behave differently.' Authority exists so that everyone can feel more alive. When life has been injured, we have to enter into dialogue until it is restored.

Personal conscience is formed through this dialogue with authority, which needs time. It is a matter of confirming the good in each person and encouraging it. Authority is an awakener of conscience. A few years ago, I used to know the deputy to the boss of a big firm. He would laugh as he told me about the long meetings when all the heads of departments had to listen to the boss telling them what to do. When he was away, my friend the deputy took his place. He would sit down with the department heads and ask them about their problems and questions, and through discussion they would seek out solutions. Here are two very different ways of exercising authority. The first consists in declaring the law, what ought to be done. The second consists in attentiveness, and helping others to become more responsible and creative. It is the capacity to listen and to dialogue which makes the difference between power and the authority exercised by a true shepherd. Even when one of the department heads is failing to observe the structures, dialogue is still important, together with a reminder of the essential rules.

Timothy Radcliffe spoke about this in connection with his term as Master of the Dominicans between

1992 and 2001. He was asked, I remember, if he had often been called to defend his brothers before the Congregation for the Doctrine of the Faith. No, he said, because when delicate questions came up, he called in the brothers concerned and they took time together to talk and discern the truth. So Timothy's authority was based in attentiveness and dialogue. Of course, he had occasion to exercise power when someone refused to accept an essential element of faith. But even then, the limits can be made clear within the context of dialogue: 'It seems that you don't recognise the Church's faith here. What do you think we can do about this?' How can ruptures be avoided? Surely it is by developing interaction between the pole of authority and the pole of power.

When power becomes compulsive and needs to impose superiority, this is dangerous. There is danger too when the person with power is fearful of encounter and dialogue. If the boss gives his heads of department to understand that he alone has the truth, dialogue becomes impossible. Power which is not lived as authority in dialogue becomes menacing.

Everyone in a position of individual power needs to watch out for this drift. But so do whole groups, when they fear that their institution's reputation is involved. In the situations of paedophilia at the heart of the Church, the defence of prestige and the fear of losing power have led people to lie and to deny the truth. Power becomes dangerous when it seeks to impose itself at any price, because no form of power can create structures of humility and mutual attentiveness. Mgr Pierre Claverie, Dominican and Bishop of Oran in Algeria, who was assassinated in 1996, emphasised the importance of dialogue, but even more, the crucial role of encounter. His work meant a lot to the Church in Algeria. Timothy Radcliffe had the same attitude in his long meetings with his brothers. Encounter creates communion, and from there truth can be born.

At what moment does the exercise of power become abusive? First of all, when fear of losing it invades the individual or the group, and they feel threatened. The Catholic Church, for example, fell victim to an atavistic fear of communism; I referred to this in Chapter 1. Under the Vichy government in France, young people demanded that the bishops affirmed freedom of conscience over the imposition of forced labour which obliged women and men to work in Germany. The bishops – with one or two happy exceptions – never did this. In their eyes, the danger came from Russia, not Germany. Marshal Petain was considered a 'good Catholic': to obey him was to obey God. Was it fear, ignorance, lack of information or inability to discern that prompted this reaction? Hard to say. What were the proportions of prudence and fear? In the gospel of John, the chief priest says that if he does not condemn Jesus, the Romans will destroy 'both our holy place and our nation' (Jn 11:47–48). Should truth not have primacy over fear? This is the price of true prudence. The French bishops were caught in fear; the high priest was defending his truth ('holy place')? Too often organisations and established institutions fail to question themselves: they cling to self-preservation without counting the human cost. Personal consciences and human lives are sacrificed on the altars of ideology and power.

To exercise authority, we have to know when to
speak and when to remain silent. Waiting for the right
moment to speak presupposes an inner clarity. Thus
Jesus waited for 'his hour', the right moment, to
speak truth (Jn 2:4; 7:6; 12:23; 13:1). Cardinal
Cajetan, the commentator on Aquinas, said that a
priest who had been suspended, and so was forbidden
to say Mass, could do so with a witness if he knew, in
conscience, that he was innocent and the two could
keep this secret. The reasoning for this was that if it
became known that the priest was celebrating Mass
in spite of his suspension, it would either create a
scandal in exposing those who had unjustly con-
demned him, maybe unwittingly, or expose him to
criticism. It is extremely subtle. Cajetan's argument
says this: the priest accepts a judgement which he
knows to be false, while also affirming his personal
conscience and seeking to avoid open criticism and
scandal which may hurt himself or the judges. Scandal comes from a disordered act which creates a
public shock. This can be necessary when it is the
revelation of a truth which can be remedied if

known. Sometimes for the good of the individual or the authority concerned it is good to avoid the public shock, especially if there is no remedy to be taken. It is not always easy to determine when the act should or should not be divulged.

Sometimes decisions are dictated by ignorance. The leader of a community, for instance, may be responsible for someone psychologically fragile who is capable of lying about serious matters. Without specialist psychological help, the leader might be in danger of seeing only the spiritual and moral aspects of the situation, glossing over the individual's vulnerability and fears. To be able to take just decisions, especially when they affect people who are fragile, leaders must be open to other disciplines and specifically take advice not only from inside their institution, but also from capable external specialists. Leaders have the duty to listen to and dialogue with professionals, to take time to consult them, and to reflect and discern, so that they do not wound and crush the vulnerable person.

How is someone with responsibility to react when faced with provocative actions that could erupt into scandal? In such situations, I think it's good to create a sort of 'crisis unit'. Of course the leader should first meet with the individual concerned and dialogue with them. Then a small group made up of a doctor, a psychologist and another member of the community could create a place of safety for listening, dialogue and discernment of the problem. This could also become a place of healing, because no authority can forget their obligation to work towards understanding what will be healing for the individual concerned. This safe place will ensure that the story doesn't erupt into a media scandal, in a necessarily simplistic and rigid form which never takes into account the individual's story in all its complexity. Such an eruption cannot help either individual or institution – on the contrary. The 'crisis unit' ensures that the question is neither ignored in silence nor covered up by spiritualising it.

What are these safe places and when is dialogue needed in different situations? These are vital questions for people who carry responsibility today, if they are to exercise an authority which is both educative and healing. The questions are demanding, because it is not enough to fall back on the rules; finding answers depends on remaining attentive to individuals, to situations and to the Holy Spirit. This takes a lot of skill, humility and prayer, as well as openness to the advice of well-informed people.

The way appointments are handed out in some institutions sometimes amazes me. There is no dialogue before the decision. The person concerned may learn about their new appointment through an impersonal letter or even an official circular. This is an abuse of power, unacceptable and inhumane. At l'Arche, we decided to take up the challenge posed when people changed roles. We concluded that we wanted someone who carried a lot of responsibility to be accompanied by a team of three people during the changeover, because this is always a difficult transition. This team helps the person concerned to discern the direction they want to go in, by discussing their wishes, different possibilities and the financial implications. We can't simply ignore this need for dialogue and discernment.

These are elements that make the difference between the exercise of power and the exercise of authority. They can be particularly important when someone has to leave a position with which they feel deeply identified. To tell them that they must learn to take on their suffering and live through this period of loss and mourning is not enough of a response to their difficulties. The real spiritual challenge is to understand the underlying human problem. When someone gives up a responsibility in which they have felt so deeply rooted, in some ways this is for them like living through a death. Then the important thing is truly to accompany them through their mourning so that little by little they can turn towards a new life. In many such delicate transitions, a place of knowledgeable dialogue and discernment can bring about a personal turnaround and a deepening of communion. By contrast, a lack of pragmatism or want of true and compassionate attention can only lead to disaster.

The exercise of authority is a vocation from Jesus. He reveals himself as gentle and humble, profoundly loving towards those whose personal conscience may sometimes become obscured, and who are also human beings with their whole history and all their fragilities and difficulties. Jesus lived humiliations and abandonment at the cross. Leaders are not there to make people live the cross but rather to accompany them in their suffering and their growth towards fulfilment.

CHAPTER FIVE

FROM ISOLATION
TO COMMUNITY

If community has always been seen as important in the life of the Church and society, today it is crucial. I would say that it is now absolutely necessary for the growth of a healthy exercise of authority, and of faith and love as well.

What is a community? Praying and living together, eating at the same table and obeying the same rule? These are not enough to create true community, no more than the skeleton which provides a structure that may or may not allow each member to grow freely in love. But skeletons need to be enfleshed with bodies and hearts: we have to love each other as Jesus loves us (Jn 13:34). People will know that you are my disciples, says Jesus, by the love you have for each other. Community is the place where communion is made manifest and where we grow in communion. It is a place of deep humanity. To be a true community we must, from time to time, come together and share something personal, something of ourselves. 'My grandmother is dying, so if you see me looking despondent, it's not about my feelings for you.' 'I'm reading this really exciting book – it's helping me to live!' 'I've got a sore foot and I'm finding it so difficult to walk.' Each person should feel able to share something they are living, because if we are to love someone, we have to know them personally. This doesn't mean unpacking ourselves and spilling out all our secrets. It's more about a certain quality of sharing which includes the body with its frailties and wounds. We humans aren't only 'pure spirit', rational intelligence or will, cut off from the body and its needs. We are also fragile hearts in vulnerable bodies. We need the love and support of our brothers and sisters.

Don't we also need regular times of personal sharing about our experience of faith and the community's vocation? We can share around a page of the Gospel, each person saying what the passage evokes in them; without this becoming a long discussion or a lecture, it allows us to exchange what we are living spiritually and humanly. This sort of sharing of the Word was important in all the first Christian communities. It brought together very different people: Jews and Greeks, landowners and slaves. To the great astonishment of observers, these very different people were clearly happy to be together. They loved each other. They came together around the Word and the breaking of bread, and for a teaching. Two things struck the observers of these first communities: their joy and the quality of love between them, however great their differences, and their non-proselytising love and care for the poor of their districts and towns. These two things, because everyone could see them, were 'signs'.

Sometimes in religious life, a theology of community and vocation can be quite out of touch with the reality of life and the personal conscience. I remember a nun who was seriously depressed and was sent to l'Arche, where she stayed for a few months. She had been ordered, as an imperative, to be vigilant not to lose her vocation. But the essential had been ignored. When she came to see me, I told her: 'Nothing can separate you from the love of Jesus.' Another nun, from another community, had been told that if she left she would lose her soul. How can people say such things? Membership of a religious community cannot become an absolute in itself. The danger is that 'vocation' becomes an ideology. There has to be discernment for each person and acceptance that as someone evolves, the community may no longer be their place. And it has to be re-emphasised that whatever their decision, they can always be with Jesus, given to him. The most important thing is that individuals grow in freedom and inner joy, with the support and guidance of genuine accompaniment.

Recently, I had a very beautiful experience of community life at a prayer meeting of an Evangelical church. Someone got up and said: 'David has been in

prison for two months and I've been to visit him.'
Someone else: 'Mary has sore legs and that's why she
hasn't been able to come to church.' And so on.

In this way, people were brought into the life of
their community even though they were physically
absent, and we prayed for them. Communion among
these people was made manifest through a reciprocal
attentiveness and a care for each other that was very
concrete and very personal. This was a true community, where you could feel that each person belonged
in mutual love.

People with authority at the heart of a community
need to experience true personal growth and transformation. They need to know how to turn not just to
professional experts, but to 'people of wisdom'. At
l'Arche, we worked for years with a psychiatrist who
was a lot more than a good professional: he was a real
wise man, deeply respectful of each person. Many
people consulted him about their personal journeys;
they brought their important questions to him; they
asked his advice about whether this was the right
place for a particular assistant or whether they would

be better somewhere else. Life's most important questions are often complex. We need someone outside of the community, someone who can give advice that is not just competent, but impartial and clarifying.

Life in community can sometimes be horrible! This person or that can get on our nerves with their rigid attitudes, their emotional needs or simply by being who they are. Thérèse of Lisieux used to find one sister in her Carmel 'disagreeable in every way'. Sometimes they had to work together, but on occasion this proved too much for Thérèse. She fled. We can guess that this sister provoked levels of anguish and aggression in Thérèse that she didn't want to show. Sometimes community life can evoke a level of rejection, even hatred, of the other that is hard to overcome. One of Jesus's commandments says: 'Love your enemies. Do good to those who hate you, speak well of those who speak ill of you and pray for those who persecute you' (Lk 6:27). But it is impossible to love an enemy with human strength alone; it needs a strength that comes from God. Through the prophet

Ezekiel, God promised to change our hearts of stone into hearts of flesh by putting his Spirit into us (Ezek 36: 26–27). Community is where we discover our own fragilities, wounds and inability to love. We cannot get away from the negative in ourselves: we have to face it. To live in community and grow in love takes a gift of the Spirit as well as real work on ourselves.

The ecumenical communities of l'Arche in Australia used to have gatherings which they called 'host and guest'. First a Protestant would describe to the community and its friends how their own church had made it possible for them to know and love Jesus more fully. Then a Catholic responded to what they had found striking in this story, before sharing their faith experience in their own church. The Protestant would in turn respond to what had touched them in this: the devotion to Mary, for instance, or to the Eucharist. That was it: no discussion or debate, simply each person speaking of what had seemed wonderful in the other. This is what living in community is about too: seeing the positive in the other and accepting them as they are, with all their human difficulties. To love a brother or sister means recognising them as a person; it means revealing to them their own beauty.

Is the peace that ended the war between Protestants and Catholics in Northern Ireland a real one? These two communities have never truly entered into dialogue. The war between those who fought for a united Ireland and those who fought to stay part of Great Britain may have ended, but there is no real peace. There have been too few mutual encounters around differences in appearance, accent, what people eat or drink. So there is no real communication because cultural differences are too embedded. Real peace is a communion of hearts which demands encounter and genuine work on oneself.

What can be done to help people accept and love each other? That is today's major challenge! Different cultures remain based in social hierarchies, just as they did in the time of Francis of Assisi. Then, the nobility lived in their own exclusive part of the city, while the bourgeoisie, those engaged in different trades, lived and worked in their own quarter, within their own culture. The poor, the lepers and the destitute lived outside the city walls and did what they could to survive. These differences have always existed, and we still throw up walls to define our own closed worlds. But communion between different people demands the very opposite: a shift, a turn-around, an upheaval that breaches those separating walls to make possible an encounter with the other in their humanity. Francis and Claire of Assisi left the closed world of their social and religious milieu to live the culture of the Gospel.

These old social barriers may seem archaic. But have they disappeared? Absolutely not. A few years ago I was travelling to Chile. When we were going from the airport to Santiago my driver pointed out to me: 'On the left, there's the huge slum of Santiago – and on the right the homes of the rich, defended by the police and the military. And nobody crosses that road between them'. So there still are the two worlds, separated by a simple road, two cultures separated by psychological walls built of fear. St Paul tells us: 'Jesus is our peace; he has made one people out of two, breaking down the wall which divided them, and ending their hatred through his flesh' (Eph 2: 14–16). A community inspired by Jesus is called to become a place of encounter and unity. That means not only receiving a new spirit, but working on oneself.

One of the aspects of our contemporary world that I find most striking is the unhappiness and anxiety that centres on work, financial problems and fear of unemployment. There is tension at the heart of families, as the older generation feel the young have fewer and fewer ideals. What are most people really seeking? It is joy, and joy is what is so terribly missing. It is buried under the understandable preoccupation with staying in work and holding together the fragments of life. But it is tarnished even more by the frustrations built up by the images of an unattainable consumer culture which dominate commercial centres, television and the internet. There is no joy in any of this, yet it is joy for which people most thirst. Joy springs up when people work together for unity and peace. But today's social systems pervert community life and relationship in general. Different categories of people are put into different places: hospitals, residential accommodation, nursing homes. Most of the time, these centres are completely professionalised and specialised. These days, it is becoming more and more complicated to create a l'Arche community. The imposition of so many regulations and standards has its value. But it makes community life more difficult.

How can we create centres which aren't just professionally competent but where hearts can be touched and people can give themselves to each other through relationship? How can we build places where encounters like that between Peter and Mamie become possible, where these in turn become the source of life-giving energy and where real sharing can happen?

The joy of living together felt by the first Christian communities is celebrated in the Acts of the Apostles: the joy of sharing with the poor rang out like good news for everyone (Acts 2: 46–47). It can seem hard for a believer to be happy in the face of all that is going on in the world today. But isn't there still the joy of belonging to a 'body'? And even in our time, it is still joy that attracts us. Jesus says: 'I give you my joy so that your joy becomes complete'. The new evangelisation, it seems to me, doesn't consist only in seeking personal conversion through announcing Jesus; it must also invite people to enter into a community where people love each other. This means offering places where people celebrate together and experience a feeling of belonging. Joy comes from this feeling of belonging to a community, of feeling good together despite our differences, of feeling that we are no longer alone with our problems and griefs. The main means of evangelisation today is in little communities where people of different origins are happy and joyful together and love each other. These can offer an experience of the community's faith and vocation and of what it feels like to share at a personal level. We can offer the sense of belonging that everyone seeks to women and men of different ages and abilities, to people who are disabled or handicapped, to those who have Alzheimer's. The invitation to participate in the life of the community, to taste the joy of being together, makes possible the discovery that in the depth of the human being there is a need to celebrate life and to feel at ease in each other's company.

There is danger in the sense of isolation which is so widespread today: the growth of sectarian movements is also a response to the huge need for belonging. A sect is a community which is closed in around the figure of a guru and built on fear. People join because they are afraid – of loneliness, of feeling lost, of going to hell – and they stay there for the same reasons, for fear of the consequences if they leave. These groups are shut off behind concrete walls. A healthy community must be open and help each of its members to grow in a real inner freedom. Hospitality is vital for any Christian community, because it teaches it to welcome each person as they are, humbly and with respect. In our l'Arche and Faith and Light communities, we try to keep a balance between freedom and belonging. A place of belonging enables each person to feel safe and supported, and to live in harmony with their brothers and sisters; the community's rituals and celebrations express and strengthen this feeling of security. But too much emphasis on belonging can stifle freedom, just as too much freedom can lead to insecurity and anguish. Belonging should allow each person to become themselves, and to grow in freedom and human maturity. And for that, the awakening of the personal conscience, about which I wrote in Chapter 2, is indispensable.

What is it that unites a community? Isn't it its mission, which is also its goal? If there is a lack of clarity about the community's vocation and purpose, it is harder to live together. The early Christians found unity in the breaking of bread (Acts 2:46). Today, the breaking of bread has become so ritualised that we have forgotten this communion of hearts and mutual support. We need to re-find a joyful expression of Eucharistic communion which leads to a communion of hearts, and to create communities whose heart is universal, inclusive, and neither exclusive nor excluding. When it comes to communities of faith, we have to educate our consciences to a vision of God as the universal Father, who loves each person. Jesus is there for everyone; each person is called to get to know him, whether he is named or not. A culture of welcome, especially of the most disadvantaged, can bring everyone out of themselves into a dynamic of opening, communion and sharing.

The strength of l'Arche is that its mission is deeply human. L'Arche is about helping people with a disability discover their human value, their personal beauty and the importance of their own individual conscience. It is about helping them to see that behind their disabilities, their culture and their human problems, lies their unique self. Some of our communities – like those in India, Bangladesh and Palestine – are made up of people of different religions, human beings who rejoice together and sometimes weep together. At the heart of l'Arche's life is the joy of communion.

It saddens and frightens me when I hear people speak scornfully of Muslims without ever having taken the time to meet and listen to them. These people cannot accept that the Muslim faith helps people to live humbly and openheartedly towards others who are different. Our societies seem to have reached a deadlock: hard to go forward and impossible to go back. So many barriers are being thrown up to separate us from each other! Perhaps it takes a completely unpredictable upheaval to bring people together. I remember for example a winter in Montreal, when there was a power cut, and therefore no heating. The temperature was 20 degrees below, something had to be done. People created emergency shelters and distributed hot meals. They came out of themselves and got together in the town halls and other places that still had heating. They met each other, got to know each other, shared what they had and responded creatively to the crisis and to individual needs. Ten days later, the power was restored, and everyone went back to watching television. All that sharing and creativity just stopped. These extreme situations help us realise just how hard it is to redirect our steps, change the way we live and find places of community where we talk, share and celebrate life together.

After the devastating earthquake in Haiti in 2010, our l'Arche community there could no longer stay in its house because it was too unsafe. Its members had to join the village people in the tents, and despite huge difficulties, they managed to create a community together. Of course we can't wish for disasters so that people are thrown into coming together and working for solutions! Rather we should be following the intuition of someone like Dom Helder Camara in Brazil. For him, the future of the Church lay in the vitality of small, church-based communities, centred on the Eucharist and the welcome of the most disadvantaged. In a country like Brazil, it's not a question of ensuring that everyone comes to the Eucharist – unless the Eucharist means an event which gives people the strength to live alongside others with all their difficulties, in the humility of Jesus. The danger is that the Eucharist becomes simply a rite which gives an identity, guarantees a certain morality and favours people of a particular social class, at the risk of engendering different sorts of exclusion. That would be to forget one of Jesus' most striking teachings, which could apply equally to the Eucharist: when you offer a meal, don't invite

your parents and friends, your kinfolk or your neighbours, but invite the people who are poor and
maimed, blind and lame (Lk 14:12–14). Then you
will live 'a beatitude'.

In our societies, we need to discover small and
joyful communities where people are welcomed to
eat together, and gradually move towards the Eucharistic table, sign and presence of the poorest and
weakest one of all, Jesus crucified. These places of
humanity and communion are sources of life; they
bring new hope.

What is it that helps such communities come into
being? In places where people can feel they belong,
where they can be related and open, we can perhaps
rediscover a real sense of the frailty of the human
body. Some religious groups which are centred upon
spirituality have lost touch with this. But a sense of
the body's frailty can teach us to become part of
another 'body', made up of small, vulnerable but
interdependent communities. When the strong and
the weak live together, a compassionate love is born:
mutual help passes through weakened bodies. The

stronger help the old to get up and go to bed; they help those with a disability to shower, to shave, to get dressed. The weaker people awaken tenderness in the hearts of the stronger; they transform them into 'real' people, capable of true compassion. The stronger reveal to the weaker their deepest human value. So each person, weak or strong, becomes someone uniquely valuable. At the heart of society's ills is a call to create more community. And Christians are surely invited to dare take the initiatives which will shine a new love into our troubled world.

CHAPTER SIX

FROM STRENGTH
TO VULNERABILTY

A coming together of those at the top of society and those at the bottom: that is what we need today. In his own time, Jesus was the sign of something new – a promise of joy, liberation and universal peace. Jesus – the Word made flesh – united in himself the height and the depth: he lived in his very person the union and the unity of heaven and earth, the infinite and the finite. As David Ford, the Anglican theologian, has said: the wisdom of Christianity lies in the meeting between the cry of God and the cry of the poor.[1]

Living in l'Arche with people who have profound disabilities, I have discovered the fragility, the vulnerability and the humility of Jesus himself. This is not just the fragility of his body, but the vulnerability of the one who knocks at the door and runs the risk that it will remain closed to him (Rev 3:20). This is his cry of love. In the first Alliance between God and his people, weakness sometimes appeared as a sign of personal or collective punishment. In the Gospel, when Jesus is asked whether the Galileans or the people of Jerusalem crushed by the accidental collapse of a tower were more sinful than others (Lk 13:1–5), or whether a man is blind from birth because of his own or his parents' sin (Jn 9:1–3), he denies forcibly that there is any connection between weakness and disability and either sin or wrongdoing. There is only the vulnerability, exposed in what is sought in relationship with us.

The fragility of Jesus offers something extraordinary: a new love and liberation of the heart. And he found his offer refused: the rich, the well to do, turned down his invitation to the wedding feast (Mt. 22). I am always moved by the words of Jesus to his apostles after his teaching on the Bread of Life: 'Will you also go away?' (Jn 6: 67). I hear the tears in his voice and his great vulnerability, the humility of the one who offers himself and is abandoned. What does Jesus offer? Communion, which can only happen because he brings himself in his weakness so that we can live in a relationship of love with him. His loving heart is wounded. Weakness is not something to be overcome or rejected: it can become the very means by which we can live a greater communion.

The humiliation that the Church is experiencing today in several countries could also become an opportunity for it to recognise the vulnerability, wounds and fragility of some of its ministers, and so an opportunity to reconsider how it prepares them to live their vocation. It is fortunate that these facts of the Church's life have been revealed. Now we can face and accept this wrong which has been hidden for too long. The first step is to reveal the truth and re-establish justice. But we are all called to take a further step: to recognise our own fragility and accept our own humiliation, so that we can bear witness to a new presence of God in a humiliated and humble Church, of which we are all part.

I have listened to people who have been sexually abused in their childhood and I have been horrified, overwhelmed and touched by the immensity of their suffering and its human and psychological effects. I cannot understand Christians who insist that such stories are all got up by the media and the Church's enemies. This is simply a refusal to hear reality, so that they can hide behind the idea of a Church which will always be 'perfect'. We are faced with an enormous challenge. There can be a projection of the all-powerful God which makes it hard to accept weakness in all its forms. There can be a refusal to accept the humiliation of fragility, of wrongs done, of the small number of vocations, of the number of people who leave the Church, of the difficulties of speaking of Jesus in today's world. There is indeed something anguishing in our current situation. But instead of transforming this anguish into a peace that rests on acceptance of reality and confidence in Jesus, we risk persisting in wanting to show that the Church must become stronger than ever. Benedict XVI, during his visit to Great Britain, opened a new path by his attitude of gentleness and humility, and his call for cooperation between Church and State. Weakness allows us to discover new things; it reveals aspects of the Gospel which have not yet been explored.

We are entering a new world, in which there will be a much higher proportion of fragile people who live with the illnesses, disabilities and psychological weaknesses associated with age. There is a growing imbalance between people who are active and those in need of support and financial help. In a situation where there are not enough financial resources, there will be a risk of a systematic recourse to euthanasia, which runs counter to a vision of the dignity of human life. We can even fear there will be a general-ised use of pre-natal screening for genetic illness, followed by abortion. Isn't this a new sign and a new challenge for Christians? It is not a question of simply declaring ethical principles; there has to be action. If we don't react by taking refuge in outmoded dreams of glory, we can find a new way of living the gospel message opening before us.

How can Christian men and women be persuaded to turn towards the weakest of our societies, not simply to look after them and evangelise them, but to meet them and be evangelised by them, to receive from them the Gospel we need today? There was a time when the monasteries of St Benedict revealed a presence of God. Doesn't our own time demand a new way of living, in communities of love where the weak are welcomed and reveal a new presence of Jesus?

Something new is coming to birth with the crowds of poor and vulnerable people which our societies, our way of life and the development of medicine have created. An encounter between strength and weakness can make possible an interaction through which the weak can find a certain security and develop, and the strong can learn to accept their own vulnerability and discover the real meaning of human life. This reciprocity can engender a sense of belonging centred on the least strong and create places of communion and a new way of life.

My own hope is that many diocesan synods and meetings take as their theme 'The poor as source of change and evangelisation'. If this is to happen, it seems to me that we need an explicit dialogue between the social doctrine of the Church, diocesan life and a spirituality which can inspire our actual reality, and truly transform us through an encounter with those who are weakest and most vulnerable. Disciplines like sociology, theology, philosophy, psychology and economics need to be drawn into this dialogue to express and clarify, from their own viewpoint, which way we should be going. It is through this sort of mutual listening that we will be able to discern, in the name of social justice, a will to act and be transformed. And we need to look for realistic solutions to problems. Befriending a person with a disability or alcoholism isn't going to provide an instant solution to their difficulties. But this friendship can lead to a mutual transformation by touching the place where God lives in each one of us. We can then begin to work *with* people who are fragile instead of simply *for* them. We can dare to work together towards a new world, in which problems can be faced, one by one, with the help of different disciplines, and in which people will truly listen to each other with a new humanity.

In the Church and in society, more and more people are discovering the wisdom of the poor. It's not a question of 'doing good' to them, but of learning from them, discovering and honouring the gifts they can bring, through and in a relationship of friendship with them. Isn't this the message of Father Joseph Wrezinski and the movement ATD Fourth World? In his book *Les Pauvres sont l'Église*, Father Joseph expressed this clearly: if we become close to the poor, we are transformed.[2] This is also the message of those who work in palliative care, accompanying people at the end of their life. It is the message too of those who listen to the simplicity with which children speak of their love of Jesus. It is the message of l'Arche and Faith and Light.

I'm struck when I read that there are more than a billion Catholics in the world, and more than two billion Christians. That must make it a wonderful place to live in! But it isn't, and at the very least we can ask ourselves why our world is not more humane. Has our faith truly reached into our bodies and hearts, or is the Church in danger of closing itself off by over-identifying with its rituals? Without a real and deep transformation of hearts, faith changes nothing in life; it engenders neither a new vision nor a new world. The encounter with the poor and those who are vulnerable brings a transformation that is simultaneously spiritual, social and profoundly human. We have to find a new wisdom, new ways of life, based on this experience.

I think we are living in an auspicious time. Our societies are not going well, crises are multiplying. Some people think that this is preventing us from finding hope for the future. But perhaps it's the opposite: this is our chance to think about the world in a different way, discard outmoded assumptions and become creative. Sometimes fear and mistrust of today's possibilities leads to a retreat into old structures rather than an embrace of the new truths, discoveries and skills of the human sciences. These structures can become rigid and use up a great deal of energy in resisting change; if they were dismantled, there would be space for something else to come in.

Benedict XVI was deeply concerned to proclaim a new evangelisation in wealthy and developed societies. This wealth is seductive, and sometimes more dangerous for the Christian soul than the persecutions which made three million martyrs in the course of the twentieth century. I remember talking to a Pentecostal bishop in Russia about Christian unity, and him telling me: 'In prison, we were all united, but now we are divided.' Adversity, persecution, humiliation and financial crises can lead us to become more humble and stronger in our faith. The vulnerability of Christians who are persecuted can lead them to encounter each other and unite around what they share as essential. Perhaps the crises to come could awaken the hearts of Christians from different churches to come together, listen more faithfully to the Holy Spirit and bring good news to the poor.

Isaiah offers us a signpost on this new – and so ancient! – road of transformation through encounter with the poor. This, says the prophet, is what is pleasing to God:

> To lose the bonds of wickedness,
> to undo the thongs of the yoke,

to let the oppressed go free,
and to break every yoke.
To share your bread with
the hungry,
and bring the homeless poor into
your house;
when you see the naked, to cover
him,
and not to hide yourself from
your own flesh.
Then shall your light break forth
like the dawn,
and your healing shall spring up
speedily;
your righteousness shall go before
you,
the glory of the Lord shall be
your rear guard'.

(Is 58: 6–8)

And the prophet goes on to emphasise how extraordinary the fruits of opening our hearts will be:

Then shall your light rise in the
darkness
and your gloom be as the
noonday.
And the Lord will guide you
continually,
and satisfy your desire with good things,
and make your bones strong;
and you shall be like a watered garden,
like a spring of water,
whose waters fail not.
And your ancient ruins shall be rebuilt;
you shall raise up the foundations
of many generations;
you shall be called the repairer of the
breach,
the restorer of streets to dwell in.
(Is. 58:10–12)

The renewal of the Church and the new evangelisation are carried through encounters with people who
are broken by suffering and isolation.

CHAPTER SEVEN

FROM SECRET
TO MYSTERY

These days, the word 'secret' can have a negative connotation. But the Vatican Council's text on conscience, referred to in Chapter 1, can help us deepen the concept. *Gaudium et Spes* evokes the personal conscience as the secret of the individual: 'Conscience is the most secret core and sanctuary of a man. There he is alone with God.'[1] This dimension of the human being can in no way excuse us from legal duties: these are of another order. But conscience implies intimacy of time and place. I'm sometimes overwhelmed by today's multiple means of disseminating news and comment. People want to publish

'secrets' without discriminating between and respect-
ing these different outlets. Some news needs to be
made public and even official, especially to expose
illegalities; some should be communicated only
within the family and community; and some again
belongs to private life, to the closest friendships or
most intimate relationships. In the same way, we
should respect that which belongs to revealed faith
and should be declared by the Magisterium, and that
which concerns the growth of a human being, about
which the human sciences and people of wisdom
have taught us so much.

When we speak of love, the word 'secret' is not
enough: we have to speak of 'mystery'. That is why
the first chapter of the Constitution *Lumen Gentium*
is entitled 'The Mystery of the Church'. A secret can
be divulged, and then there is nothing further to
discover. But a mystery is never exhausted; we can
always plunge deeper into it. And I say 'plunge'
deliberately, because a mystery is something we
inhabit: we don't contain it, it contains us, because it
is larger than we are. A secret dwells in us. But we

dwell in a mystery. A mystery can contain all of us, each with the singularity and uniqueness of our own secret, in relationship with the secret of others.

A secret is about uniqueness and difference. How are we to live together, become one body, as long as the differences between us seem to constitute a menace? L'Arche exists in many countries, in the midst of many ethnic and religious tensions. I am very aware of cultural differences and all the prejudgements that come with them – between Saxons and Celts, Tutsis and Hutu, Serbs and Croats, Israelis and Palestinians ... There can be real walls around our hearts which prevent us from encountering those different to ourselves. We so quickly exaggerate the tensions and differences, cementing in the name of a greater security our own cultural identity and a dominant and dominating mentality; we continually feed opposition, fear and hatred in the name of security.

How can we transform a social and international vision based on rivalry into a vision of the human family as being like a body, with each culture bringing its own gift to enrich the whole, making it more beautiful and true? How can we destroy the walls that separate one from the other, the walls around our own hearts, and our human groupings? Strong cultures give individuals identity and safety: without them, don't we risk falling into the anguish of insecurity? How can we help Celts and Saxons to encounter each other? How can we help people from the slums and those in the rich suburbs to cross the road that divides them and to meet?

Jesus came to bring together in unity all the dispersed people of God. He came to bring peace. After eating with Lazarus, he left Bethany and went down to Jerusalem, where he was acclaimed as the king of Israel (Jn 12:1–15). This was the fulfilment of the prophecy of Zechariah: 'Shout aloud, O daughter of Jerusalem! Lo, your king comes to you; triumphant and victorious is he, humble and riding on an ass … And he shall command peace to the nations; his dominion shall be from sea to sea' (Zech 9:9–10). This is the triumphant entry of the one who will bring peace to the world. Immediately afterwards, John mentions the Greeks who want to see Jesus. And

Jesus declares (or does he sigh?): 'The hour has come for the Son of man to be glorified' (Jn 12: 20–23). The royal triumph is transformed into a realisation of his coming betrayal and death. Until this passage in John's Gospel, the disciples of Jesus saw him as the one who would liberate the Jews from Roman oppression. Jesus chooses the moment of the arrival of the Greeks who want to believe in him to show that he has come to liberate each person, however closed off in their own ego-centricity and the walls of their culture and group. He is the Saviour of the world.

So we begin to penetrate the mystery. By his descent into poverty, Jesus is going to unite all peoples and achieve the impossible: transform rivalry into communion. He is going to transform the hierarchies in which each group, each person, seeks the highest and strongest position, into a body in which each one, from the strongest to the most vulnerable, can find their place.

The mention of the Greeks is followed by Jesus's solemn declaration:

Truly, truly, I say to you, unless a grain of wheat falls into the earth and dies, it remains alone; but if it dies, it bears much fruit.

He who loves his life loses it, and he who hates his life in this world will keep it for eternal life.

If anyone serves me, he must follow me; and where I am, there will my servant be also; if anyone serves me, the Father will honour him.

(Jn 12:24–26)

In the vision of the journey to peace that Jesus opens, there are three complementary roads, three paths of humility which lead people beyond their ego. The first refers directly to him: from death will come a huge fecundity. There is a life-force in the single little grain which will produce forty or a hundred others. From the death of Jesus, from his pierced heart, a new presence will spring; from his death he will bring life to the multitude, the life of the Holy Spirit. The gift of the Holy Spirit will lead individuals and also the Church from the security of belonging to a defined culture to a new security, in which hearts of stone will be transformed into loving hearts of living, loving flesh. This is how people from different cultures will be able to encounter each other and become one. As Paul says: 'He is our peace who has made us both one, and has broken down the dividing wall of hostility' (Eph 2:14).

Jesus is speaking of his own death, but his words apply equally to everyone who wants, through him, and in him, to open themselves to peace by bringing down the barriers between cultures. The Beatitude for the peacemakers is that they will be called sons of God (Mt 5:9). Once transformed by giving up the security of the group, they will live like their elder brother Jesus. Just as the young Etty Hillesum realised the necessity of integrating death in order to live fully, we too have to integrate all our deaths: the deaths of the heart, our humiliations, our losses and mourning. From these losses, by the gift of the Spirit, will spring a new fecundity. John Paul II said: there is no peace without justice, and no justice without forgiveness. To descend into the insecurity of humility in order to open ourselves to peace implies forgiveness. Isn't this one of the last words of Jesus on the cross: 'Father, forgive them'?

The second path to peace has to do with our compulsions. Our tendency is to want to 'rise above', to show that we exist and are better than others; we want to be admired and recognised as important. Without this recognition, who are we? To live, and live in the eternity of God's life, we have to accept not 'succeeding' within our own culture. If we are to take the path of humility and live in eternal life, in God's own life, we have to suffer loss. We have to give up wanting to have the last word to prove that we are better than the rest. This struggle with our compulsions is a long journey, as I know from my own experience, my own anguish and violence. The late Patriarch of Constantinople, Athenagoras, invited us to disarm, and recognised what a struggle this is: 'The hardest war is the war against oneself. We have to arrive at renunciation. I waged this war for years and it was terrible. But I am disarmed. I no longer fear anything, because love chases fear away'.[2] To become a peacemaker implies becoming disarmed, to live in humility and above all in the life of God.

The third path to peace is to serve Jesus in the poor, to live among them. The Lord said, through Isaiah: 'I dwell in the high and holy place, and also with him who is humiliated and lost' (Is 57:15). In every religion and culture, there is the presence of the 'lowliest'. At least a billion and a half women, men and children live today in huge and wretched slums. To be with those who are humiliated, pushed to the margins of society, is to live in the house of God, to live with Jesus. In living the culture of the Gospel, we leave the security of our Western structures. This is what the brothers of Taize were talking about when they created a pilgrimage in Bangladesh for people with a disability from different religions.

> We are discovering that those who are rejected by society on account of their

weakness and their apparent uselessness are a presence of God. If we welcome them, they lead us progressively away from an over-competitive world where people need to accomplish great things, towards a world of hearts in communion, a simple and joyful life, where you accomplish little things with love. Our presence in Bangladesh aspires to be a sign that the service of our vulnerable brothers and sisters opens a road of peace and unity. Sometimes it is the poor who bring us together. Welcoming one another in the rich diversity of religions and cultures, serving the poor together, prepares a future of peace.[3]

This encounter, this life with those who are wounded and humiliated, is a source of happiness. It brings good news. I can say that since I no longer hold responsibility in my community, my life at l'Arche has brought me new joy: each meal with my house-hold is a blessing, a beatitude, of the sort spoken of in

Luke's Gospel (Lk 14:12–24). There are glances, smiles, words, laughter, events that move us; we can live a love which is neither too close nor too distant. Even moments of aggression between two people can find a place in this ample space of freedom and connection. Someone may be angry with another who touches something painful in their own history, but such tensions are tempered and made relative by the overall atmosphere of joyful shared emotions. A feeling of togetherness and of a common bonding seems to sum up this unique setting and its trans-forming encounters. We understand each other because relationships with ourselves and each other are at a good comfortable distance. There is no struggle to appear above the other or to be recog-nised. Like tenderness, our communication passes through the body: a glance, a wink, laughter, a ges-ture, moments of celebration and forgiveness. We are not looking for power; we are looking for joy in being together, wherever we are placed in society's hierar-chy. It is this life together which reveals their true value to both people with disabilities and their assistants. Of course it isn't always simple and easy; real life is more complicated. As well as the light of the Gospel, there are all the fears that can come up from the darkness. But the vision of Jesus is there, the beatitude of sharing a meal with the poor. This beatitude is the doorway into the kingdom of Jesus.

The path of peace is about 'serving Jesus'. This brings me to the question of interpretations of the scriptures. There are many legitimate ways to interpret a saying of Jesus. We can fly very high or choose a reading which comes down to earth, into real life. To read and deepen John's gospel, for example, we need the Paraclete, who reminds us what Jesus said and will lead us to the full truth of that Word for today (Jn 14:26). The Paraclete introduces us to communion with Jesus, and through him, with the Father. David Ford, in his book on Christian wisdom, gives good criteria and guidelines for interpreting the scriptures. Read the Scriptures for God himself, he says, for his glory; read them guided by the faith of the Church as it moves through the drama of history; read them with the saints who went before us; never separate the Old Testament from the New; start with the most obvious meaning, but be open to others; read in the belief that the four Evangelists are telling the true story of Jesus; read together with others in a Christian community; read with members of the society in which you live; read together with believers from other religions; read with a view to friendship with all; read rooted in your own life, renewing the reading from the reality of experience. And lastly: read the Gospels to grow in love and union with God.[4]

In Chapter 13 of his Gospel, John tells us that after the moment of agony before his death, the death which would yield such fecundity for the world, Jesus humbles himself. He is on his knees: like a slave, he washes the feet of his disciples. It is a shocking gesture, and Peter can't accept it: 'You shall never wash my feet!' But Jesus washes the feet of his disciples with tenderness and love. He touches their feet, not out of duty like a slave, but lovingly. And he tells them that they too should do what he has done, in memory of him. They should set out on a path of poverty, humility and service. Isn't this a radically new path? These men who are at the origin of the Church must become servants of the excluded and the poor. These are the people who are calling to them. The way of the Church is a way of humility, oriented towards service to those who are excluded and socially insignificant.

There is in today's rich societies a diffuse thirst for spirituality – that is, for a road that will lead to human fulfilment and a union with God, the source of all life. From the Gospel of John emerges a deep spiritual unity which is not attached to any particular tendency, religious order or specific group. It is a spirituality which gives freedom – but a freedom lived in community. This spirituality invites us to become like Jesus, love like Jesus, kneel as he kneels, gently and humbly. This has a depth which many had not even suspected. John brings this spirituality to light and each one of us is called to follow it and to grow continually in this flow of love. Jesus wanted this spirituality of John to be very clear: Peter has his vocation in the unfolding Church, but John has his, which will be to reveal this spirituality of union with Jesus himself (Jn 21:20–23).

Reading John's Gospel, we can see how the disciples gradually discover who Jesus is. Until Chapter 13, he appears as strong, inspiring, admirable, an envoy of God, the Messiah who will manifest the signs of his power. Until now, the only time he has spoken of love for the disciples is when he is speaking of the family at Bethany. And then, as Passover approaches, John reveals who Jesus is and how he loves: 'having loved his own who were in the world, he loved them to the end' (Jn 13:1). He loves them to the fulfilment, to the completion, to the extreme and beyond. It is by his love that he reveals who he is. Until now, the signs have been only of the power of God; there has been no full revelation of his mystery. The mystery of God is that he is there, in front of the disciples, on his knees, humble and fragile, the very opposite of powerful. Jesus responds to questions not as a teacher but as a friend who has been hurt: 'Have I been with you so long, and yet you do not know me, Philip?' (Jn 14: 8–10). Peter's violence and refusal to have Jesus wash his feet are signs of his incomprehension of this human and divine weakness. And then when Jesus will not defend himself and so will be put to death, Peter will cry: 'I do not know him' (Jn 18:17). He does not know this fragile and loving Jesus who wants to live in him, as in us all.

In John's Chapter 13, the three principal actors take their own positions when faced with this frailty and humility of Jesus. Peter is strong but loyal. John communicates with him in this frailty and Judas fears love. Already in Chapter 6 and again in Chapter 12, faced first with the Bread of Life and then with Mary of Bethany's anointing of Jesus' feet, Judas has shown that he cannot bear the smallness of love: he wants to follow a Jesus who is strong and glorious.

John's approach is very relevant now for several reasons. The first is precisely this smallness of God, still insufficiently explored in the history of Christian spirituality, often hidden behind the omnipotence of God. Here we can talk about the powerlessness of the all-powerful, the powerlessness of love. It isn't to deny God's omnipotence, for example, to assert that he could not have acted through history without his messengers. It is a question of love. Only love can go so far as to say: 'I knock at the door and wait' (Rev 3:20). 'God is love' (I Jn 4:8). Only love can suffer when it is not loved. All of philosophy and particularly theodicy shows suffering as a lack. If God is perfect, he can lack nothing and so cannot know suffering. But isn't there another theology and spiritual hypothesis, which understands suffering not as a lack, but as a superabundance of love?

The second reason for the relevance of John's gospel is that it speaks clearly about the Holy Spirit in relation to fragility. Since the Council of Trent, the Holy Spirit has hardly been evoked by the Church; the first encyclical on the subject was Leo XIII's in 1897.[5] More recently, since the Vatican Council, charismatic movements have connected with the tradition of St Paul and the gifts of the Spirit. In these movements, however, there is no distinction between the differences of language and vision carried by the words Spirit and Paraclete. In all the translations, *spiritus* evokes breath, energy, inspiration: a divine force. The best translation of Paraclete, *paracletus*, seems to be Comforter or Consoler, and this must always imply a *relationship* with those who are weak and afflicted (Mt 5:4). The Paraclete is given in the fragility of anguish, when we feel alone, abandoned and lost. It is given as a mother who comforts and loves her children (Is 66:3), so that we can live a love which is patient, forgives all, believes all, hopes all and endures all (1 Cor 13:7). The theology of the Spirit in John's Gospel is that of the Paraclete, a life-giving presence which brings life to those who suffer. This presence is subtle. The Paraclete moves at the level of small experiences which have nothing dramatic about them and are found on the margins of the official channels. This action is like an underground stream, a consolation lived by the 'afflicted', often in a hidden way (Mt 5, 4).

Finally, the Gospel of John speaks to our times because it opens us to mystery. Jesus said to his disciples: 'He who sees me, sees the Father' (Jn 14:9). This was so that they could dare to say: 'They who see me, see Jesus'. Isn't this the road that we are called to take? Jesus tells us that he calls us not servants but friends. Those who eat his flesh and drink his blood dwell in him as he in them: 'If someone loves me, they will keep my word and my Father will love them and they will dwell in Him.' 'Those who live in me and I in them will bear many fruits'. 'Live in my love' (Jn 15).

The last words of Jesus on the Cross, just before his death, are addressed to Mary and his well-beloved disciple: 'Woman, this is your son. This is your mother'. From this moment on, Mary belongs to John: she becomes his treasure. Mary is called to bring Jesus to birth in John. Jesus will live in him.

A prayer of Cardinal Newman, who was beatified by Benedict XVI in September 2010, opens us to this mystery:

> Dear Lord, help me to spread Thy fragrance
> everywhere I go.
> Flood my soul with Thy spirit and life.
> Penetrate and possess my whole being so
> utterly that all my life may only be a

radiance of Thine.

Shine through me and be so in me that every soul I come in contact with may feel Thy presence in my soul.

Let them look up and see no longer me but only Thee, O Lord!

Stay with me, and then I shall begin to shine as Thou shinest; so to shine as to be a light to others.

The light O Lord will be all from Thee; none of it will be mine;

It will be Thou, shining on others through me.[6]

Cardinal Newman's prayer was adapted by Mother Teresa for her own use and that of her Missionaries of Charity. This prayer is also mine, but I am far from living it. To live in Jesus and let Jesus live in me is not a pious or devotional thought. It means living the vocation of Jesus: announcing the good news to the poor, liberating the imprisoned and oppressed. It means entering our world's struggle against the forces of evil, working for justice and peace. Allowing Jesus to live in me implies a true death to myself.

At the end of this book, I dare to suggest that the mystery to which we are called is to live like Jesus, who became small and weak. He is hidden in those who are humiliated, in the poorest, the foolish and the weak of our societies, all those whom God has chosen to confound the intellectual and powerful of the earth – and also, it has to be said, of the Church itself. To enter the Kingdom, Jesus said, we have to become as little children (Mt 8:1–6). People with a profound intellectual disability, like some old people, certainly have adult bodies, but often they have the hearts of children.

These pages have brought us to the threshold of a great mystery. We can't deny that today our lives and those of our societies are shot through with absurdity. But when love passes through absurdity, it has the power to transform it into presence. And in this presence we can live. 'Abide in my love' says Jesus (Jn 15:9). Abide with Jesus as he washes the feet of the poor.

This is the path he shows us, for the feet of the poor are also the feet of Jesus.

'Behold, I make all things new' (Rev 21:5).

NOTES AND REFERENCES

1   All quotations from Vatican II documents are from the official English version at http://www.vatican.va/archive/hist_councils/ii_vatican_council/ unless otherwise stated.

INTRODUCTION

1   *Translator's note*: Throughout, 'the Church' refers specifically to the Roman Catholic Church.

2   Second Vatican Council Closing Speeches and Messages. Official English version at www.ewtn.com/library/papaldoc/pbclosin.htm

3   *Translator's note:* There are many different ways of referring to people with an intellectual impair-

ment. In the UK, we still often hear of people with 'learning difficulties', in the USA, of those with 'developmental disabilities'. I have opted for 'intellectual disabilities', because this is the term used by the author and because it is favoured by Inclusion International and Faith and Light, both widespread international organisations.

4   All quotations from the Bible are from the *Revised Standard Version, Catholic Edition*.

5   Ash Barker, *Slum Life Rising: How to Enflesh Hope within a New Urban World*. Urban Neighbours of Hope: UNOH Publishing, 2012. www.unoh.org.

6   Address of the Holy Father Pope Francis, 16.3.2013. Official English version at www.vatican.va.

7   Homily of the Holy Father Pope Francis. 19.3.2013. Official English version at www.vatican.va

8   Urbi et Orbi Message, Easter 2013. Official English version at www.vatican.va.

CHAPTER 1: FROM HUMILIATION TO HUMILITY

1   *Author's note*: I have deepened my understanding of this subject through reading a book about the martyrs of Algeria: Martin McGee, *Christian*

Martyrs for a Muslim People. New York: Paulist Press, 2008.

2 Luigi Accattoli, *Quand le pape demand pardon*. Paris: Editions Albin Michel, 1997, pp.75–87.

3 Quoted in Henri Tincq, *Jean-Marie Lustiger, Le cardinal prophete*. Paris: Editions Grasset, 2012, p.196. English translation: www.dialogue-jca.org/Repentance_des_eveques_de_France.htm.

4 Julia Kristeva and Jean Vanier, *Leur Regard Perce Nos Ombres*. Paris: Fayard, 2011.

5 *Gaudium et Spes*, 16:1.

6 *Translator's note*: This passage does not seem to be included in Etty Hillesum, trs. Arnold J Pomerans, *An Interrupted Life*. London: Persephone Books, 1999. My translation comes from the French edition: Etty Hillesum, trs Philippe Noble, *Une Vie Boulversée*. Paris: Editions du Seuil, 1995. 2.10.42, p.233.

CHAPTER TWO: FROM CONFORMITY TO CONSCIENCE

1 See for instance Benedict XVI's discussion with journalists on the plane to Fatima, 11.5.10; his homily on the Solemnity of Sts. Peter and Paul, 30.6. 10; his address to the Roman Curia, 20.12.10. www.vatican.va.

2 *Lumen Gentium*, 8. www.vatican.va.

NOTES AND REFERENCES

3   Benedict XVI and Peter Sewald, *Light of the World*. San Francisco: Ignatius Press, 2010.
4   M. Scott Peck, *People of the Lie*. London: Arrow Books, 1990.
5   *An Interrupted Life*, 3.6.42, p.190.
6   Benedict XVI, General audience, 1.7. 09. www.vatican.va.
7   Official English version at http:// www.vatican.va/holy_father/benedict_xvi/ encyclicals/documents/hf_ben-xvi_enc_ 20051225_deus-caritas-est_en.html paragraph 14.

CHAPTER THREE: FROM EXCLUSION TO ENCOUNTER

1   *Gaudium et Spes*, 16:1.
2   Julia Kristeva and Jean Vanier, *op. cit.*
3   *An Interrupted Life*. 12.7.42, p.218.

CHAPTER FOUR: FROM POWER TO AUTHORITY

1   *Gaudium et Spes*. 4:1.

CHAPTER SIX: FROM STRENGTH TO VULNERABILITY

1   David F. Ford, *Christian Wisdom: Desiring God and Learning in Love*. Cambridge: Cambridge University Press, 2007.

2   Joseph Wresinski, *Les Pauvres sont l'Eglise*. Paris: Editions du Cerf, 2011.

**CHAPTER SEVEN: FROM SECRET
TO MYSTERY**

1   *Gaudium et Spes*, 16:1.
2   Olivier Clement, *Dialogues avec le Patriarche Athenagoras*. Paris: Fayard, 1976, p.183.
3   www.taize.fr. Meeting in Kolkata, Meditations by Brother Alois, 6.10.2006.
4   David F. Ford, *op.cit*.
5   *Divinum illud munus*. www.vatican.va The Holy See- The Holy Father – Leo XIII – Encyclicals.
6   www.jesustower.com/Prayersd/ prayersjesusnewman.htm.